SEA WARFARE

SEA WARFARE

WEAPONS, TACTICS AND STRATEGY

H. P. Willmott

With an Epilogue by
ADMIRAL OF THE FLEET THE LORD HILL-NORTON, GCB

ANTONY BIRD PUBLICATIONS

First published in 1981 by
ANTONY BIRD PUBLICATIONS LTD
Strettington House, Strettington, Chichester
© H. P. WILLMOTT 1981

ISBN 0 917319 02 5

Designed by John Mitchell
Printed in Great Britain by
Clarke, Doble and Brendon
at Plymouth

TABLE OF CONTENTS

THE PLATES

Opinions and arguments in this book are purely those of the author and are not endorsed by the Ministry of Defence or The Royal Military Academy, Sandhurst.

GLOSSARY

ACV/SES	Air Cushion Vehicle/Surface Effect Ship (hovercraft)
A/S	Anti-submarine
ASDIC	Sonar
ASW	Anti-submarine warfare
c.i.f.	Carriage, Insurance and Freight
CPSU	Communist Party of the Soviet Union
CV	Heavy carrier
CVA	Heavy carrier (term used before 1975)
CVL	Light carrier
CVN	Nuclear-powered heavy carrier
CVS	Anti-submarine carrier
CVV	Medium carrier
DDH	Helicopter-carrying destroyer
ECM	Electronic counter measures
EEC	European Economic Community
EEZ	Exclusive Economic Zone
ERW	Enhanced radiation weapon (the neutron bomb)
f.o.b.	Free on board
FY	Financial Year
GNP	Gross National Product
g.r.t.	Gross Registered Tons
Liner	A cargo-carrying ship working a route or line, not a passenger ship
LPD	Landing Platform Dock (an assault ship)
MARV	Manoeuvrable re-entry vehicle*
MIRV	Multiple independently-targeted re-entry vehicle*
MRV	Multiple re-entry vehicle*
NATO	North Atlantic Treaty Organisation
n.m.	nautical mile (equal to 1.15152 statute miles/1.84243-km)
OTH	Over the horizon

*   Strategic nuclear missiles began as single-warhead ballistic missiles that in time developed a MRV capability. This was an ability to deliver three warheads in a grouping around a single target. Subsequently MIRVed missiles were developed. This involved an incoming missile shedding a number of warheads against separate targets. MARV missiles have the same capability but are able to manoeuvre while in flight and are not, therefore, strictly ballistic.

RAF	Royal Air Force
ro/ro	Roll on/roll off
SALT	Strategic arms limitation talks
SAM } SA-N }	(Naval) Surface to air missile(s)/missile system
SCS	Sea control ship
SLBM	Submarine launched ballistic missile(s)
SSBN	Nuclear-powered submarine with ballistic missiles
SSM } SS-N }	(Naval) Surface to surface missile(s)/missile system
SSN	Nuclear-powered fleet submarine
SUW-N	(Naval) surface to underwater missile(s)/missile system
VSS	V/STOL (or Vistol) support ship
V/STOL	Vertical/short take off and landing*
VTOL	Vertical take off and landing.

*   The term increasingly used in the place of V/STOL is STOVL, Short take off and vertical landing, which seems to be the trend in naval development. Because of V/STOL or STOVL capabilities the ships that carry them do not have to turn into wind to launch or recover aircraft. Comment in the text to the effect that ships with such aircraft (e.g. HMS *Invincible*) are not able to keep pace with a task force therefore may not be accurate, but the comment is in terms of design speeds technically correct.

CHAPTER I

SEA POWER:
TO DETER AND DEFEND

Leaving aside the obvious fact of human mortality, a participant in the Battle of Salamis in 480 BC could have fought at Lepanto in AD 1571 with relatively little difficulty. Similarly, one of Drake's sailors who fought the Spanish Armada in 1588 could have fought the Franco-Spanish fleets at Trafalgar with equal facility. Yet a sailor who fought at Trafalgar could not have gone into action at the Dogger Bank in 1915 or Jutland in 1916, though the admirals of 1805 would have understood quite easily the conduct of British and German commanders at these two engagements. Moreover, they would have grasped the general manner in which both Britain and Germany fought one another at sea between 1914 and 1918.

But a sailor who fought in the great battle between Christendom and Islam at Lepanto would have had some difficulty in adjusting to the demands of the 1588 campaign that was fought around the coasts of the British Isles between protestant England and catholic Spain. This is in spite of the fact that a mere seventeen years separated the defeat of the Armada from the crushing Christian victory that crippled Moslem naval power for generations. Equally, a sailor of the First World War would have had certain problems in adjusting to the new demands of naval warfare after 1939 while a combatant in either or both world wars could well be literally 'all at sea' in dealing with the problems of naval warfare since 1960. The pace of technological change is not a constant.

These simple notions point to the subtle but critically important relationship that exist between strategy, tactics and technology. What links or separates sailors of different eras and races is the relationship they had with the matériel of their time. What binds the Greek and Persian of Salamis with the antagonists at Lepanto and what links the sailors of 1588 and 1805 is the thread of continuity: no fundamental changes in naval warfare took place in the intervening years. What divides the various ages of naval men are the technical changes that took place. These changes led in turn to a drastic alteration in methods of fighting at sea.

1

Methods of conducting operations (i.e. tactics) and technology are indissolubly linked because tactics are determined by weapons, and weaponry is the product of industrial and technological sophistication. The arbiter of tactics is generally the most powerful weapon in existence at any given time, but one of the oldest military clichés in the world is that while weapons and tactics change, men, geography and strategy do not. Strategy, the basic principles involved in the conduct of war, by the terms of this argument, outlives tactical developments and changes in weaponry.

A formidable array of historical evidence exists to give support to this view. Yet it is difficult to resist the notion that in the last three or so decades a series of developments resulting from the process of de-colonialisation and the world-wide emergence of sovereign independent states and the development of nuclear power both as a means of propulsion and destruction, have wrought qualitative and quantitative changes in the conduct of war that account to a fundamental rewriting of traditional strategic concepts. In no case is this more true than with regard to naval warfare because by granting navies a strategic nuclear role, navies - or at least the navies of the four great oceanic powers - have secured functions of defence and deterrence that are basically at odds with one another if for no other reason than that the weapons that are used to discharge one function cannot be used to carry out the other.

This has not always been the case. Historically, naval power has been both a means of defence and deterrence at one and the same time, the ships of the day being able to act in both capacities. To explain the fundamental dichotomy between the present aspects of naval power involves a definition of sea power and an outline of its development. Here one runs into an immediate problem. The story of sea power and sea warfare, indeed our view of navies and the role they play, since it is historically based, is one that has been conditioned by the British experience. British naval supremacy existed for about three centuries and during that period, though defeats were suffered at various times, the British triumphed in every war they fought at sea and used the sea for their own purposes. The concept of sea power has therefore been established with a British perspective that has stressed the importance of undivided command of the sea. French, German and Japanese views have taken second place to this concept of sea power that developed in the seventeenth, eighteenth and nineteenth centuries at a time when maritime communications were superior in every way to those overland. Neither of these conditions - the permanency of British naval supremacy and the advantage of sea communications over those by land - exist any more. The navy that took over the British mantle in the course of the Second World

War, and whose existence has been the cornerstone of the Pax Americana and the underwriter of western democracy, the US Navy, no longer enjoys a position of clear superiority over its most serious challenger. Hence the concept of sea power, and in particular the concept that lays emphasis upon the indivisibility of command of the sea, has undergone considerable amendment even within Britain and the USA.

To understand this process of change one must consider the functions and sinews of naval power. Sea power, in its historical and traditional role, has been the means by which nations have attempted to ensure in wartime their retention of maritime rights automatically enjoyed in times of international peace. The prime consideration in these matters has been to ensure immunity against physical invasion and raids from the sea. In the case of Britain but not, for example, in the case of Germany, in two world wars the secondary aspect, the maintenance of seaborne lines of communication and the safety of oceanic trade, has equalled and even eclipsed this prime function in immediacy and importance. No other tasks compare in importance to these, the defensive functions of naval power. The offensive use of maritime strength - offensive operations against enemy coastlines and his lines of communication - normally cannot hope to be successful unless and until the defensive aspects of sea power have been secured.

But, of course, the role of navies in war is but one aspect of their overall functions. Sea power, as it has been conceived in Clausewitzian terms, has been, and still remains, an instrument of state power and policy. Leaving aside the role that navies have had in peacetime of suppressing piracy and slavery and of policing maritime resources, and turning attention solely to aspects of state policy in the context of *realpolitik,* sea power has always been a means by which a nation could apply pressure, discreetly or otherwise, on another nation. Force has always been the final arbiter between states, and sea power is but one aspect of force. Whether under conditions of normal peace or in a crisis, sea power has been a means of pursuing state interest. It has been and remains a means of ensuring a physical presence even in areas geographically remote from the state itself and in this role it is acceptable since it is flexible, relatively slow in becoming effective (i.e. it buys time) and, critically, is generally less threatening than the deployment of other means of force. Mobilisation of armies, for example, is far more threatening than the deployment of naval force, and history has often shown mobilisation to be an irreversible process. The use of naval force, however, has less immediate dangers attached to it. The imposition of a blockade against Cuba in 1962 by the US Navy as the means of enforcing American will over the presence on the island of Soviet nuclear weapons is such an example. The use of naval power by the Americans was the least dangerous option that presented itself, and the slowness with which events unfolded at sea gave time for both sides to conceive and implement a rational response to a highly dangerous situation. The American action was no less effective for its being, in effect, a 'low profile' act.

Sea power, therefore, has been a means of exerting pressure on an enemy or even another state that is not involved in war. It has been the means by which a nation has sought to force another to desist from a course of action or to adopt policies not necessarily in full accord with that nation's perceived interest. As an instrument of force, as a means of carrying out a national objective, perhaps the most pertinent single illustration of the deterrent role of navies is provided by the Imperial German Navy at the turn of the century. One of the best studies of the Imperial Navy is entitled *Yesterday's Deterrent,* a title which recognises that the Imperial Navy was built primarily as a deliberate act of policy in order to reduce the political and military options of another party, in this case Britain, though it must be admitted that other considerations - of national prestige and the belief that a battle fleet was indispensible to the dignity and status of a great power - were at work. In this case the German intention was to build a navy powerful enough to be such a threat to Britain's freedom of choice vis-à-vis other powers that she would be forced either into alliance with Germany or benevolent neutrality. This policy, of course, failed, and in failing revealed the truisms that force and military factors alone are not the determinants of national strategy and that sea power is not identifiable solely in terms of fighting fleets. Likewise, the American attempt to deflect Japanese attention from south east Asia by deploying a deterrent force in 1940-1941 at Hawaii failed to achieve its objective, and, like the construction of the Imperial German Navy before it, the policy of deterrence proved self-defeating. It was not a question of the lack of force as such: more precisely it was the miscalculation of the role of force in being able to achieve its objective that was all-important.

What differentiates the deterrence role of yesteryear from that of today lies in the ability of modern navies to destroy the homeland of an enemy, by the use of strategic nuclear weapons. Historically, the ability of navies to destroy objectives on land has been extremely limited. But in the modern age the navies of the four major maritime powers have the ability to strike with devastating effect throughout an enemy homeland. This is the element of novelty. It has called into being a concept of security - against war rather than defeat - that deliberately rests on the notion of assured destruction as a means of ensuring if not peace then the avoidance of open and general conflict.

The combination of these new concepts and weapons has profoundly altered naval affairs. In purely nautical terms the increased range of modern weapons is part of the process that has enabled navies to strike at targets beyond the horizon. Historically, if one accepts as a rough rule of thumb the (very inaccurate) notion that organised naval warfare dates from Salamis, then about 98 per cent of all naval warfare has been conducted between ships unable to fight except when in sight of one another. For about 90 per cent of this time action could only be joined when ships were either physically touching one another or so close that the difference was negligible. Only in the first quarter of the present century did ranges begin to open, and only in the second quarter did it become possible for warships to engage in battle without seeing one another. In this situation it is a matter of indifference if the enemy was one or one hundred miles beyond the horizon: the horizon itself marks the qualitative change in the conduct of naval operations.

Initially, of course, the means of striking beyond the horizon was the aircraft. The British attacks at Oran and Taranto in 1940 and the Japanese at Pearl Harbor in 1941 pointed to the clear development of a means of projecting offensive fire-power deep into sea areas that, in hitherto orthodox terms, were controlled by another power's surface units. But if that development itself represented a profound (if gradual) change in concepts of naval warfare, then one matter is clear. The destructive capability of aircraft remained limited.

This stands in total contrast to the present time when the American and Soviet navies have a virtually unlimited destructive capacity and the navies of Britain and France have the ability to inflict considerable and perhaps an unacceptable level of destruction on the Soviet homeland. This movement into total destructive ability has been deliberate. Both the Americans and Soviets have systematically created navies whose major efforts are directed to ensure a permanent capacity to destroy the other's heartland as a deliberate act of policy.

Any examination of this situation inevitably and unfortunately brings into question the whole nature and workings of strategic nuclear deterrence - and the word 'unfortunately' is used deliberately because the concept is complex. In part the difficulty that surrounds the subject is caused by the jargon used by 'experts' to confuse the layman and, perhaps, themselves. The policy of deterrence, as noted, involves the deliberate pursuit of a policy of restraining an adversary by threatening a penalty should he persist in a given course of action. In the context of strategic nuclear weapons the penalty is the infliction of a level of damage such that any gain that an adversary might hope to achieve would pale into insignificance when set against the

5

destruction of his homeland.

In order to be effective deterrents must possess certain character-istics. A deterrent must have the capacity to inflict such damage, and it must be technically and politically credible. A deterrence policy is unworkable if, for any reason, the nuclear arsenal is very limited in its size, if it cannot be relied upon to work in the event of the need for its use arising and if no one believes that the possessor would actually use it under any circumstances. The part that navies play in this lies in the fact that at the present time the two super-powers rely on a three-fold means of delivery, the TRIAD system. This is the combination of land-based, air-launched and sea-borne nuclear weapons, the triple means of delivery being considered necessary as the means of ensuring that an enemy pre-emptive strike could not succeed in destroying its adversary's means of retaliation. By the dispersal of the means of delivery an 'assured second-strike capability' is guaranteed. The nuclear arsenals of the USA and the USSR are overstocked to the extent that both have the means of destroy-ing each other several times over. By dispersal and possession of an 'overkill' capacity, even the most successful pre-emptive strike would still leave untouched sufficient forces to launch a retaliatory strike that would destroy the aggressor. For a super-power contemplating a pre-emptive strike a 90 per cent guarantee of success is not enough: the 'miss-ing' 10 per cent would be enough to put his country back into the Stone Age. As a deterrent the submarine-launched missile is all-important because it alone is endowed with an extremely high level of immunity from detection and hence destruction. Land-based missiles are normally static and vulnerable, even in hardened silos. Bombers are slow and relatively vulnerable. Cruise missiles, rather than destabilising the balance of terror and inviting attack, will in time make pre-emptive strikes ever less likely because of their smallness, cheapness, numbers and their ability to fly below ground-based radars. Because submarines have the expanses of the ocean in which to hide, because they have the ability to evade and outrun any surface ship on the high seas with ease and because their weapons are aimed at civilian as opposed to military targets, submarines are at the heart of any policy of deterrence. The price that a pre-emptive attack would be forced to pay would be the destruc-tion of civil targets from a secure second strike: the civil population of the super-powers are the hostages for the good behaviour of their governments. As long as submarines retain their high degree of immunity from detection and destruction and as long as an incoming missile has a reasonable chance of striking its target(s), the sea-borne deterrent is secure. It is widely believed, however, that in the next decade some breakthrough in anti-submarine warfare will take place, and it is also thought that technology will develop to the point where it will be possible to destroy missiles en route to their objective without airburst.

Such developments *may* lie in the future, and we can do no more than note the destabilising effect that such breakthroughs would have upon the validity of deterrents if, and when, such breakthroughs take place. But deterrents at the present time involve an element of defensive capability. The current NATO doctrine of flexible response involves conventional ground and air forces playing a crucial role. Defence, the ability to fight a conventional war as a means of trying to prevent an escalation of conflict to the point of strategic nuclear release, is in fact at the heart of flexible response. At sea, nuclear-powered submarines with strategic missiles (SSBNs) cannot be used in any other context except that of deterrence or, in the event of a deterrence policy having failed, the agent of strategic nuclear destruction. Their one and only role is in the strategic context, and they can no more take part in the battle for command, control or denial of the seas to an enemy than they can carry out a 'showing the flag' role in peacetime: their specialisation makes their diversified employment impossible. The superiority of nuclear-powered submarines, whether SSBNs or hunter-killers (SSNs), over present-generation surface ships - advantages in detection and target acquisition ranges, weapons and performance - is such as to give rise to the dictum of nuclear submariners that in the next war there will be two types of ship, submarines and targets. Surface ships cannot hope to play more than a marginal role in the strategic nuclear sense because of their manifest inferiority to nuclear-powered submarines. It may very well be, however, that in the event of war between the super-powers and their supporting alliances, both might try to use their surface ships in box formation in order to deny enemy SSNs access to certain sea areas, simply because their own SSBNs would be in those areas. This might be particularly the case with regard to the Soviet Northern Fleet which may choose to keep its *Delta*-class SSBNs near the icepack in the Barents Sea and employ their surface ships across the Greenland-Norway gap in order to prevent NATO SSNs getting amongst their latest and best strategic submarines.

Such hypotheses, of course, are merely speculative. To return to more immediate matters, it almost goes without saying that in peacetime and in the context of war below the nuclear threshold, i.e. in limited wars, the surface ship is all-important and the SSBN is essentially irrelevant, and these facts lie at the basis of the dichotomy between the present aspects of naval force. At either end of the naval spectrum there are warships whose functions and characteristics make their operations mutually exclusive, but both are vitally important and virtually omnipotent in their own fields of activity.

7

But it is no more correct to consider naval power solely and simply in terms of fighting ships than it is to see war and confrontation as the only or even the main manifestation of conflict and hostility between states. Sea power and inter-state rivalry are both like pieces of rope: they are made up of various strands, all of which are vital to the cohesion of the whole but only one of which is uppermost at any given time. Both the various aspects of sea power and the range of inter-state confrontation have to be considered in order to understand the significance of recent developments at sea.

One problem in writing about sea power is that romance, legend, art - the aspects that are pleasing to the eye and the appreciative senses - have traditionally focused attention on just one aspect of it. This aspect has been its most photogenic parts, the fighting ships themselves or the great captains. This is natural. History abounds with examples of ships of great aesthetic beauty - Britain's *Tiger* (of 1912) and *Hood,* Germany's *Bismarck,* the Japanese *Yamato,* Mussolini's heavy cruisers - that commanded attention even in their own life time as being the acme of contemporary technical skill. The British *Queen Elizabeth*-class battleships and later the American *Essex*-class carriers can probably be considered as ships that were very special in their own ways. Their combination of a sense of power, purpose and menace, glowering but symmetrical profile and graceful, elegant lines, made such ships as the five *Queen Elizabeths* notable even in their own time as special in their own right. The concentration on the photogenic has meant that other elements of sea power, such as geographical position and access to the open sea, the possession of forward bases, the availability of sea-borne and shore-based fleet facilities and the back-up of a powerful and sophisticated industrial base, have tended to be relatively neglected. Moreover, the commercial use of the sea is, as we have argued earlier, perhaps the most important of its aspects, and sea power, at sea, consists of various types of ships of which one type, the warship, becomes of primary importance only in war. The warship in war must defend those ships that use the sea for 'industrial' purposes, and the importance of the sea for 'industrial purposes' continues to grow.

The sea has been traditionally used for 'commercial' purposes, and indeed the sea-borne empires of the states of western Europe - such as Portugal, The Netherlands and Britain - arose because of these countries' development of trade throughout the world. For the time that these states remained great imperialist powers their empires were held together by trade. In the case of Britain, the phenomenal scientific, technical and social expansion of the eighteenth and nineteenth centuries was made possible through sea power and commercial activities; trade and earnings from insurance and transport in part funded trade deficits. For Britain this situation remains true today, and it is also true of the USSR. Though many factors have led the Soviets to press ahead with the development of a large merchant fleet, such factors as prestige and status compare marginally when set against financial reality. The USSR produces nothing, or nearly nothing, that the rest of the world needs, and what she can provide is only primary products. Oil, precious metals and timber are the three most important foreign currency earners for a state that cannot feed its own people, cannot produce enough consumer durables for its population and cannot pay for what it does get from its neighbours. The Soviet merchant fleet is the Soviets' fourth largest foreign currency earner, and its expansion and deployment on various routes has not been accidental but part of a deliberate economic policy.

But this development has not simply been an economic one. Non-commercial strategic objectives have figured large in Soviet merchant fleet development. The Commander-in-Chief of the Soviet Navy, Admiral Gorshkov, has publicly stated that the Soviets regard their merchant fleet as an indispensable arm in their overall capability in overseas ventures. Along with Aeroflot, the development of the Soviet merchant fleet and particularly her liner fleet, which provides the means of carrying military personnel and equipment to client nations, gives the Soviets the chance in future to achieve a dominant position on the principle trade routes, particularly in the carriage of strategic cargoes. This is one area of the East-West confrontation where there has been relatively little western thought and action.

The growth of the Soviet merchant fleet has to be seen in the context of Soviet recognition of the importance and vulnerability of western lines of communication, already weakened by the decline of Anglo-French power in Africa and Asia and the failure of western powers to settle on any consistent and clear programme towards Third World states. Western dependence on Africa, Asia, the Middle East and the Indian Ocean has grown rather than shrunk with the process of decolonialisation. In terms of raw materials and export markets the North Atlantic Alliance is dependent on areas outside its borders to a greater extent than has ever been the case hitherto, yet its capacity to act against an ever growing Soviet capacity outside the European area has never been smaller. It may well be that the critical threat to NATO might prove to be in continents and seas beyond the alliance region, the alliance becoming isolated and crippled at some time when the Soviets decided to use positional advantage for some political objective. No less a person than Soviet Foreign Minister Gromyko, speaking at the 1976 Congress of the CPSU, stated that the purpose of the Soviet military build-up was to deny the West options at some unforeseen crisis in the future. The Soviet build-up of a merchant fleet from 1,741 ships of 6,483,000 g.r.t. in 1965 to 3,029 ships of 15,880,000 g.r.t. and the continued expansion of the Soviet Navy must be seen in this context.

Formulating ideas about sea power at the present time is a hazardous business because of the highly political nature of the subject and the risk of being accused of scare-mongering or complacency, depending on the political views of reviewer and reader. Any examination of sea power at present is bedevilled by the obvious questions that surround Soviet strength, effectiveness and intentions. We in the West can give no answers to these questions with any degree of precision, mainly because the Soviet Union, being a closed society, deliberately does not make evidence available. Virtually every aspect of western naval policy is known because of the accountability of western armed forces to their respective legislatures. Such accountability does not exist in the Soviet system, and to accept Soviet protestations of injured innocence regarding her maritime activities is ingenuous. Soviet secretiveness and general adventurism around the world in the last decade is at the basis of any misunderstanding, if there is any, and for that the Soviets have only themselves to blame. Certainly no one in the West can understand the logic that lies behind the Soviets' building of ever more merchantmen of ever greater size when their present fleet is more than four times greater than their own trading needs and why the Soviet Navy continues to grow with ships of every type and size at a time when it is more than sufficiently large to discharge any reasonable defensive tasks that could be placed upon it.

To try to summarise any thoughts about sea power and its use at the present time is therefore difficult, but it must involve certain statements of fact and certain theoretical considerations, some of which have appeared in earlier pages. Of prime importance must be the fact that events at sea must not be seen in isolation, but in conjunction with developments on land, in the air and with regard to the strategic nuclear balance. The rise and decline of British sea power no more took place in a political and strategic void than the rise of the Soviet Navy over the last three decades has been accidental or divorced from a process that has seen the USSR secure nuclear parity and then superiority, the massive expansion of Soviet strategic and tactical air forces and the marked qualitative improvement and expansion of all arms of the Soviet ground forces.

Sea power is a rational instrument of state power, and, moreover, it is a long-term phenomenon; ships, design teams, industries, and, above all, experience, cannot be improvised. The traditional belief was that sea

10

power was essential to the status and dignity of a great power. Two world wars were in part brought about by the German and Japanese impetus, at different times, towards sea power on a global scale. Anglo-German naval rivalry in the period 1907-1914 played a major part in the outbreak of the First World War; sea power was at the heart of the outbreak of the Pacific war in 1941. But in the modern world the term 'super-state' is often used about Japan and West Germany. Leaving aside the flags of convenience, Japan probably has the largest merchant navy in the world, yet she has virtually no fighting navy and what she does have is not allowed to call itself more than a seaborne self-defence force. Germany, though divided, probably commands more respect and prestige throughout the world than at any time in the peaceful past. Yet her sea power, so important for the Kaiser and Hitler, is negligible. To some extent the lack of German and Japanese naval power can be explained by treaties forced on them after the Second World War, and by a continuing American defence commitment. But equally, the role of the German and Japanese navies today should lead us to question the traditional view of navies as essential instruments of state power.

Sea power, as we have seen, consists of many different elements, but the progressive development of fighting at sea from one dimension through to three has been critical to the emergence of concepts of sea control and denial. Command of the sea, until the Second World War considered even by those with no chance of securing it a vital concept, developed in the age of the supremacy of the surface ship. Indeed, it developed when there was no means of transport and fighting at sea except by surface ships. This century, however, has seen the extension of warfare at sea to both below and above the surface of the seas, and has seen the surface ship itself reduced from its position as the only means of conducting operations first to the most important, then to a means equal in importance to others. It has now become in a sense the least important since its value rests largely as a platform from which other vehicles - aircraft, helicopters and in future perhaps hovercraft - can operate. Obviously this process of change was gradual; artillery, the submarines and aircraft contended at different times for supremacy, as we shall see.

CHAPTER II

THE LENGTH OF AN ARM:
THE GUN

Warfare is as old as man himself, and naval warfare probably dates from the time when men first went down to the sea in ships. When, where and in what form they did so is unknown, but it would appear that the first recorded instance of the use of warships was some 5,000 or more years ago on the River Nile. Such 'warships' belied their name however, since they were not ships in the strictest sense of the word. They could not operate on the sea, and they were not fighting ships in the sense that they could function in a naval or military manner, in fact such ships were little more than rafts of reeds, pitch and lashings, elongated in shape in order that they might be steered effectively. Such craft functioned in a riverine role, supporting land forces.

But certainly by about 3000 BC men went down to the sea in ships for both military and commercial purposes. By that time both the Cretans and Egyptians had developed wooden ships that were sea-going. Both had produced ships that carried a mast, in the Egyptian case a bipod, and sail, but which also relied upon oars as a means of propulsion. In about 2900 BC the Egyptians despatched about forty such ships to Byblos in what is now Lebanon in order to carry home cedarwood, but the fact that such ships were armed would suggest that even by that time other peoples had ships that were used, and perhaps even purpose-built, to prey on traders.

There was a fundamental incompatability between merchantmen and warships, and it was this incompatability that over succeeding millenia various societies unsuccessfully attempted to reconcile. The incompatability stemmed from the simple fact that trading ships could not function efficiently as fighting ships, though their vulnerability to the latter was such that it was highly desirable that some form of fighting power should be worked into them. Despite the cost factor that was always pushing societies into trying to develop ships that could operate in both fields, merchantmen and warships each demanded specialisation because their basic characteristics differed so greatly. The merchantman's characteristics were determined by the need for cargo space. To carry unwieldy loads efficiently merchantmen had to be large, wide and bulky. By the second century AD the Romans had evolved such 'round ships' for the grain trade, and they represented the pinnacle of Roman naval engineering. It is calculated that these ships measured up to 180-ft along their waterline, 50-ft in the beam and, incredibly, drew up to 50-ft of water. In carrying capacity such ships remained unequalled until the nineteenth century. These ships had to rely on the wind for movement of course, but what was remarkable about them was that in addition to the main mast they evolved a spritsail that allowed them to beat against the wind. This technical sophistication was lost for several centuries after the fall of Rome.

The warship, on the other hand, evolved along very different lines. It was not until some time in the second millenia BC that warships began to develop, even though by that time there had been some form of naval warfare for at least 1,000 years. Throughout this time there had been fighting at sea, not a little of it directed to the protection or destruction of trade, but in a real sense in this era fighting at sea was peripheral to the warship's real role. With so many small states in the eastern Mediterranean naval power was regarded as the means of projecting military power over the sea, and the warship's real function was to transport soldiers against enemy land objectives, not to fight their way to a target or to secure 'command of the sea'. In effect warships were raiding transports. In another age the Vikings possibly became the most famous of all sea raiders, their activities ranging from the Americas to the Volga, from the North Cape to West Africa.

But if the ancients and Vikings regarded their ships as transports rather than instruments of war, it was inevitable that at various times such 'warships' encountered one another (or pirates) and engaged. Such naval actions, however, were mere extensions of land warfare with any sea-going flair and expertise subordinate to the outcome of battle between sets of soldiers that sought to board an enemy. From any point of view, but particularly from the point of view of a sailor, such encounters were invariably messy and far from satisfactory on two counts. Firstly, boarding was all but impossible in anything other than calm conditions. Secondly, even a victor could incur prohibitive losses in the course of a successful boarding. Clearly there was an incentive to seek some form of weapon so that an enemy ship could be sunk outright with very little danger of a close quarter battle in which the enemy could board.

After the third century BC missiles became available to navies. Around the start of that century catapults and ballistae began to appear, probably at the instigation of the Macedonians. It is, however, the Romans and the ballistae that are always linked together, and it is worth noting that later Roman versions on ships were capable of firing projectiles that were heavier over distances that were greater than those achieved by naval guns until the latter part of the nineteenth century. But even when such weapons became available they still remained subordinate to the weapon that dominated naval warfare for at least two thousand years.

This weapon was a copper-sheathed extension of the keel that projected several feet beyond the ship itself - the ram. The ram was intended to strike an enemy at his most vulnerable point, on or below the waterline, but throughout the era of the ram two technical considerations always had to be set against the known and proven efficiency of the weapon. A matter of yards separated ramming and being rammed, and power of manoeuvre and skills of seamanship were at a discount in the confusion of fleet action. Ramming, moreover, could prove almost as structurally damaging to the attacker as the victim. But the real problem of the ram, however, was the factor that led to its being adopted with reluctance and which was always behind the search for a dual-purpose ship. Whereas stability and safety were essential to the cargo ship that had to rely on the wind for its power of movement, the ram had to have momentum to make it an effective offensive weapon. The only way in which a ship could secure such momentum was to have some power of movement independent of wind and tide, and this could only be provided by human muscle power and oars.* This necessitated the ram having its own 'weapons platform' - the galley. Building and manning galleys, however, were very expensive because a galley, unlike a merchantman, had to move over the surface of the sea rather than cut its way through it and it had to be slim for it to be fast. Very shallow draught and sleek lines - the antithesis of the merchantman's needs - were therefore essential as far as the galley was concerned in order to reduce its total resistance to a minimum in the quest to secure the kenetic force needed to impart effective smashing power.

In the galley one sees the development of genuine naval warfare, that is warfare between ships as opposed to conflict between men who happened to be in ships. This development was naturally at the expense of the soldier. In fact soldiers became a liability because they represented

---

* In the first century AD an Egyptian, Hero of Alexandria, designed a steam engine that used steam pressure to move a turbine. His designs and calculations were quite practical, but it was not until 1897 that the turbine was incorporated in a ship. Moreover, someone whose name has been lost in the course of time, devised an oxen-driven paddle ship. This involved utilising the same principle that is used in animals being harnessed to raise water, except that they turned axles that operated paddles. Presumably the existence of slavery did away with the need for such developments which were lost to knowledge in the Dark Ages.

dead weight. The intention of the galley was always to strike and immediately reverse oars and pull away from a stricken enemy before he could grapple. Ancient societies appreciated the need to save weight and hence the need to downgrade the military component of the galley. They also came to appreciate that the optimum performance from a galley with a single bank of oars was from a ship about 85-ft along the waterline and 9-ft high, the displacement of about 22 tons being secured on a draught of about 2½-ft. The maximum number of oars that could be carried was fifty, 25 on each side; thereafter any increase in the number of oars had to be offset by increased manpower needs, material cost and the rise of the frictional resistance of the hull.

Such galleys were called either pentaconters (Greek for fifty) or uniremes (Latin for one bank), and it is somewhat strange to record that such ships survived the challenge of another form of galley that was in its physical characteristics far superior. After the unireme came the bireme, produced by decking over the unireme and incorporating another bank of oars. Such a system, however, was not really cost-effective until three banks of oars were incorporated within what was effectively two decks by an ingenious system of staggering the oars and the fitting of bulges and outriggers. This extra bank of oars more than compensated for the increased frictional resistance brought about by a lower centre of gravity caused by a draught of about 3¾-ft. A not untypical trireme measured about 100-ft along the waterline, 115-ft overall, and had a beam of about 12-ft or 16-ft over the outriggers.

The great advantage of the trireme was that whereas the unireme had a top speed of about 9 knots for a very short time, the trireme could match this, figuratively speaking, in third gear. The trireme could easily cruise at 6 knots under a single bank of oars, and at full power her 41 tons could reach nearly 12 knots. In terms of kenetic energy a trireme had three times the smashing power of a unireme.

The great disadvantage of the trireme was its cost. Its debut (possibly as a result of Corinthian ingenuity at the end of the seventh century BC) sparked off what was almost certainly the first qualitative arms race in history. Considerable historical and technical controversy surrounds exactly what happened in this race, but it is known that there were attempts to incorporate ever more banks of oars, larger numbers of oars and more rowers to an oar on ever longer ships in an effort to improve performance. It is believed that the Egyptians planned, but never built, a 400-ft tesseraconter (a forty), but the arrangement of oars for such a ship has been the subject of intense argument. It has been suggested, however, that she could have needed a crew of 4,000, which would have made her as intensive in her use of manpower as present-day

15

American aircraft carriers. In a pell-mell action a 400-ft length would have been a liability, but it was her over-intensive use of manpower that was crucial in her non-construction. What in the end condemned even the trireme was the fact that she needed a crew of about 210, of whom 170 were oarsmen. Though the trireme was the dominant weapon at sea for several centuries its demands on a very scarce resource - young, fit, highly trained and skilled manpower - were enormous, even in an age of slavery. It was far more cost effective to build three uniremes, each with a crew of sixty, than a single trireme. By the first century BC the standard Roman galley, the liburnian, was either a unireme or a bireme, and it was such ships that triumphed over the Egyptian fleet at Actium in 31 BC.

Actium represented perhaps the supreme triumph of the Romans at sea. The story of the Romans at sea was one that reflected the changing nature of warships and naval warfare. The First Punic War (264-241 BC) established Rome as the leading sea power in the Mediterranean, and this position she maintained until the fall of Rome itself more than six hundred years later. But when the Romans began they were certainly not amphibians; they were land creatures and it took many generations for them to become genuine 'maritime animals'. When the Romans began to fight at sea they had to vie with societies long versed in naval warfare. Whereas the ram was by this time the decisive weapon at sea and boarding was very clearly a secondary tactic, the Romans, in their wars with Carthage, introduced grappling hooks - mainly the corvus which was a spiked gangplank - that locked antagonists together in a fight to a finish. The Romans introduced the corvus simply in order to play to their strength, which was in the organisation and skill of their soldiers, rather than to their weakness, which was in nautical skill. In this the Romans were following, but improving, the example of the Egyptians, Phoenicians, Greeks and Macedonians. Throughout the Roman empire there was a tendency to retain a sizeable military component - of infantry, archers and slingers - for naval warfare.

Throughout the lifetime of first the Roman Empire and then the Eastern Roman Empire (Byzantium) the galley remained the supreme fighting ship. It had no rival and neither it nor the strategic and tactical uses to which it was put changed in any significant way in these eras. Strategically the Romans were innovators in that in the first century BC they systematically used their fleet to suppress piracy, particularly in the eastern Mediterranean, but with their conquest of all the lands washed by that inland sea, this need diminished in importance. After the fall of Rome, however, the rise of new powers and the challenge they posed to Byzantium led the Eastern Empire to maintain a permanent naval force to defend the Christian Empire. Apart from a specialisation of ships for battle (heavy ships) and for cruising and scouting (light galleys with single banks of oars) and the introduction (and intermittent employment) of Greek Fire as a means of burning enemy ships, naval warfare showed no significant advance in these times. Tactics were stylised and showed no improvement over those employed by the Greeks in the sixth century BC against the Etruscans and against the fleet of Xerxes in 480 BC.

In the era of the domination of the galley battle tactics were simple and unsophisticated. Antagonists invariably drew up their forces in an extended line abreast formation and charged one another, hence the traditional pre-Roman reliance on the ram as the prime weapon of destruction and the secondary importance of fighting infantry on board warships. At various times attempts were made to inject some subtlety into proceedings, the Greeks being particularly successful in attempting to avoid a straight free-for-all along the length of the battle line by concentrating their forces and attempting to overwhelm part of an enemy fleet. Such tactics, however, demanded very high levels of skill and manoeuvrability, and these were generally in short supply. Salamis was an instance, however, where the tactic was used with devastating effect, the Persian right flank being cut to pieces by a Greek force that concentrated its efforts on its left flank while its right fought a containing action against heterogeneous forces (including Ionian Greeks) that made up the Persian left. The latter in fact withdraw in good order from the scene of the battle.

Such was the enduring nature of tactics in the age of the galley that the same basic methods were employed more than two thousand years later by the Turks at Lepanto. In that battle both the Christian and Turkish fleets formed battle lines about two miles long. The Turkish left wing feinted to outflank the Christian right, commanded by the Genoan Andrea Doria, and was successful in pulling the Christian right and centre apart. But its attempt to drive through this gap and bring about an overwhelming concentration against the Christian centre was frustrated for two reasons. The Christian reserve of 35 Spanish galleys moved into the gap before the Turks could exploit their success, and the attacking Turkish left broke when it saw that not only was it going to fail but that the Turkish centre and right had been repulsed. The Turkish failure in the centre and on the right was the result of the second factor - the presence in the Christian line of galeasses.

The galeass was a galley, albeit with more than one mast, in all but one respect: it carried cannon in broadsides. The Christians had just six such ships, supplied by Venice, and these carried up to sixty guns each. Two were placed in the van of each of the three divisions that made up the Christian line. The Christian commander, Don Juan of Austria, had

17

also ordered his galleys to cut down their bows and mount guns there in order to bring against the onrushing Turkish galleys a withering concentration of firepower.

This development clearly foreshadowed an end to the galley's supremacy in war. It was not that guns were unknown at sea or that the Turks, when they closed the Christian line, encountered a totally new weapon the existence of which came as a surprise to them. What so surprised and dismayed the Turks was the sheer weight of artillery that the Christians brought to bear against them. The Christian guns battered the Turkish fleet and set up the conditions for victory in the traditional melée, characterised by boarding, that destroyed Turkish naval power for generations. The guns, however, foreshadowed more than just an end to the Moslem naval threat to Christendom: they spelt the end of the galley itself.

Guns had been at sea for more than 200 years before Lepanto, but for almost all that time they had been hand guns or light artillery pieces that had to be mounted in the 'castles' at the extremes of the ship. Theirs was an anti-personnel role since they were deployed to fire downwards into the lower areas of the ship where an enemy would make his boarding attempt. Such artillery pieces were of dubious value since they posed as much a threat to their user as to their intended victims. Their life expectancy was low, but they were undoubtedly of considerable moral value.

The decisive change in naval warfare that doomed the galley to a lingering demise - they still operated in the Baltic, Black and Mediterranean seas as late as the nineteenth century - lay in the twin development of guns to a size where they could inflict substantial damage on ships and not just personnel, and the placing of guns along the length of the ship. The first gun ports were cut into the sides of ships at the beginning of the sixteenth century by the French and English at roughly the same time.

The effect of these changes was to impose an intolerable strain on the composite material that made up the galley, accelerating a trend that was already working in favour of the evolution of the sailing ship. Heavy guns necessitated their own platform on which to fight because their weight was too great to be carried by the galley's thin decks while the sides of the ship had to be strengthened to withstand the effects of recoil and the smashing power of enemy guns. The piling on of dead weight in the form of strengthened decks and sides proved too much for oars which, in any case, were hopelessly vulnerable to gunfire. Only a sailing ship possessed the structural robustness to carry guns and withstand their effects, and only the sailing ship could embark upon the voyages of discovery then being undertaken by the nations of western Europe.

Sailing ships had existed for centuries, but it was from the twelfth century onwards that they began to evolve in northern and western Europe in a most significant manner. They had developed from ships with single masts to either three or four masts that carried a variety of sails that enabled them, unlike earlier ships with single sails, to move into the prevailing wind. It was this, plus their ability to sail in waters normally considered too dangerous for the galley, that opened up the World to European discovery and which, in the course of three hundred years, transformed Europe from the position of being the unwilling and in many instances hapless recipient of successive invasions from Asia and Arabia into the position of ruler of the world. Though not the first into the field of discovery, trading and colonisation, Britain came to be the foremost of the imperial powers by virtue of the fact that in the Age of Sail she enjoyed mastery of the one sea that controlled all the others. Domination of the English Channel and the eastern Atlantic where they met western Europe ensured British command of the seas beyond Europe that was barely affected, even by the USA, until the present century. It was this supremacy, established at source, that enabled Britain to consolidate her position by acquiring virtually every point where sea communications were forced to enter points of constriction or close to continental headlands, thus helping to sustain Britain's position in the first eighty or so years of oceanic steam. But, in retrospect, it can be seen that the sailing ship and European pre-eminence were mutually identifiable, and the passing of the sailing ship was to herald the relative decline of European power just as surely as the passing of the galley saw a shift in the balance of power away from the Mediterranean to the European Atlantic coastline.

The sailing ship with its broadsides of guns (the galleon) underwent considerable change in these three hundred years. Size doubled and, most importantly, so did the number of guns carried by the average ship. Ship silhouette changed considerably, most notably in the gradual suppression of the high 'castles' mounted fore and aft in the early galleons. These, of course, had been incorporated in order to give defenders the advantage of 'the high ground' when dealing with boarders, but the switch of guns from personnel to matériel targets did away with the need for raised decks that in any case increased a ship's wind resistance and diminished its handling characteristics. In these and various other ways - new methods of keel construction, bottom protection, the introduction of steering wheels about 1700, the suppression of the fourth mast and certain rigs - the galleon evolved, but the skills of naval warfare remained unaltered. The strategic and tactical changes brought about by the emergence of the sailing ship as the decisive element of naval warfare themselves resisted substantial revision until the time that wood ceased to be the material with which ships were built.

The most important of the strategic and tactical changes brought about by the emergence of the sailing ship was characterised by the nature of voyages of discovery. The oceanic sailing ship produced a 'long haul' navy. Galleys had been 'short haul'. Their range had been limited, and it was usual for a galley in the Mediterranean to put into port or an island overnight. The human demands of the galley meant that the ship could not be relied upon for endurance. Sailing ships had endurance, but only at the expense of the power of independent movement.

The loss of movement independent of wind and tide had a profound effect on naval tactics because it was linked to the development, or, more accurately, the non-development of the gun. The gun, a smooth-bore muzzle-loaded cannon, began as a crude, short-ranged slow-firing weapon of limited destructive power, and thus it remained for the duration of its time in service. A good well-trained crew could get off a round every minute, but apart from the heaviest of guns called 'smashers' that were fired over the bows, the ordinary gun carried in broadside was only able to inflict substantial damage if used en masse at the shortest possible range - and point-blank distance was the ideal range for a man-of-war. Guns could not be trained through arcs of fire, and therefore could only be fired at right-angles to the ship's course. Therefore tactics had to ensure that a man-of-war unmasked its field of fire before joining action and coming alongside an enemy. The tendency, therefore, was for fleets to deploy in line-ahead formation, as distinct from the line-abreast formation characteristic of galley warfare, in order to make the greatest possible use of numbers of ships and guns. The only way to compensate for the weakness and limitation of individual weapons was the use of broadsides at close quarters.

These demands immediately tested skills of seamanship. The forming of a battle line in order to engage an enemy was never an easy matter, and it was even more difficult for an aggressive fleet, seeking battle, to force an unwilling enemy to stand and fight. The technology of the man-of-war was universal, and the warships of all nations were very similar in size, characteristics and performance. Such was the basic symmetry of ship design that only the most experienced eye could tell the ships of different nations apart, and because there was so little to choose between ships and their performance, there was no substantial speed differential that conferred a specific tactical advantage on the ships of one nation over their foreign counterparts. In this situation the ability to sail as close to the wind as possible, thereby gaining as much from the wind as possible, was critical, and to take station relative to the enemy and the wind was of vital importance in the conduct of battle. To secure 'the weather gage' - to stand between the enemy and the prevailing wind - enabled a fleet to determine its battle formation and to choose its moment for joining action; but to stand to leeward, as long as the wind affected both sides equally and the line to windward did not (literally) take the wind out of the other's sails, enabled that line to turn and decline action with little that the other could do about it. The struggle between lines to secure 'the weather gage' was a recurring theme in battles in the Age of Sail, Howe, for example, spending days manoeuvring to get to windward of the French before finally doing so on 'The Glorious First of June' in 1794. Given these facts it is not hard to see why so relatively few battles were fought at sea in this era and why even fewer ended decisively. Indeed, only one battle, that of the Nile in 1798, resulted in the annihilation of an entire fleet, the French suffering total destruction. Most victories were only partial, even though partial victories could be very substantial.

Reference to Howe and 1794 reflects the fact that in the Age of Sail war at sea was primarily an Anglo-French affair in which with only one possible and partial exception, the French emerged as second best. This was in spite of the fact that French ships were generally a little superior in quality to those of the British, that France was the more powerful of the two nations and that she usually fought in alliance with one or more naval powers whereas Britain was often unaided at sea. French attentions, however, were always divided between the sea and the needs of security on land. The need for France to devote resources to the protection of her security on the Rhine contrasted with the British ability to take as little a part in continental warfare as they deemed necessary. The critical difference between Britain and France at sea, however, lay in human factors; the discipline, training and morale of British seamen and the ability and seamanship of British officers being superior to those of their French counterparts. At no battle was this more evident that at Trafalgar when the French were clearly revealed to be a second-rate enemy.

In most Anglo-French wars the French normally sought to avoid battle at sea. Their invariable concern was the preservation of their forces intact, the existence of their 'fleet in being' generally being considered more important than any transitory gain it might make by any success it might register. Geography conspired to place the French at a decided disadvantage to the British. Britain was placed across French (and Spanish) lines of communication with lands beyond Europe, the prevailing winds across the Atlantic enabling the British to blockade French and Spanish ports on the Atlantic coast in the secure knowledge that any storm that drove them off station was certain to confine the enemy to harbour. In strategic terms the French needed a fleet to tie down British resources and prevent their use against French overseas possessions, and they needed their fleet as a diplomatic counter to British power and gains when it came to making peace.

Tactically the French were as cautious as they were strategically prudent. French fleets seldom sought battle, even when they had superiority of numbers, and in action French ships normally tried to fire broadsides 'on the up' - as the ship rolled out of the sea - in order to give height to their fire. This ploy was designed to shoot away an enemy's rigging, the French objective being to cripple an enemy and thereby leave themselves with the alternatives of closing a helpless opponent or conducting an unhindered withdrawal. British practice was to fire 'on the down' - as the side of the ship began to roll into the sea - in order to direct damage into the vitals of an enemy ship. There was seldom much chance of sinking a ship through gunfire - men-of-war were notoriously difficult to sink - but damage on or near the waterline threatened to impair a ship's seaworthiness and performance, heightening the risks of the ship being wrecked or set on fire. Fire, indeed, was the real enemy of wooden ships, and flame was generally more feared than water by navies of all nationalities. But if wooden ships were largely proofed against gunfire by their thick wooden sides, they did have one weakness. Strengthened in the bows to withstand the pounding of the sea, men-of-war were vulnerable in the stern, and a favoured tactic was to come around the stern of an enemy and take him with broadside fire throughout his length. At Trafalgar the British *Téméraire* took the *Redoubtable* through her stern, killing and wounding about 200 Frenchmen with a single broadside. The *Royal Sovereign* caught the *Santa Anna* with even more devastating results. About 400 Spaniards were either killed or wounded by one raking broadside, her losses in this one part of the battle being equal to the total British losses in the whole of the battle. After such withering attacks coming alongside to board was normally little more than a formality.

Laying a man-of-war alongside an enemy was the be-all and end-all of British tactics long before Nelson made his celebrated remark that in doing so no captain could do any wrong. Few warships ever withstood full British broadsides when ships were alongside, the British invariably double- or even triple- loading their guns for the first broadside in order to inflict the greatest possible damage in the opening exchange. But to put a British man-of-war alongside a reluctant enemy was never easy, and the task of doing so was not made any easier by the limitations of British tactical doctrine and signalling.

22

The eighteenth century is often referred to as the century of limited warfare when nations, recoiling from the excesses of the wars of religion in the early seventeenth century, evolved an elaborate and almost ritualistic process in the conduct of war. The most obvious examples of this were on land where manoeuvre and battle doctrine became highly stylised with an almost mathematical and geometric precision governing deployment, movement and fire. This formalisation of war had its parallel at sea in the imposition of rigid linear formations that were difficult to bring into action at all and almost impossible to control once battle was joined. (Naval warfare was not unlike a dance at court with the dancers lined up on either side, facing their opposite numbers, sometimes to move into physical contact, but often not. This analogy can be taken further since behind the lines were the onlookers, the frigates, which could not join in proceedings. It was considered extremely bad form for a man-of-war to fire on a frigate.) But such was the severity with which admiralties imposed the line on subordinates that admirals and captains departed from it at their peril. Besides the natural hazards of combat Nelson and Collingwood took on the whole orthodoxy of the British admiralty when, at the Battle of Cape St Vincent in 1797, they broke station and placed themselves across the course of a fleeing Spanish fleet. They were vindicated by success, but had they failed at the least their careers would have been ended.

Thus in the eighteenth century there was a marked discrepancy between British strategic intentions and battle drills, both of which were offensive, and their tactics, which were very real obstacles to the forcing and winning of battle. The reason for this was the fossilization of tactical thought as a result of the issuing of Fighting Instructions. Such instructions had come into effect in the time of the Commonwealth (1649-1660) and the Anglo-Dutch wars when it had become common practice for British admirals to issue general instructions regarding their intentions before action was joined. These instructions went some way to resolving the problems of command which were almost impossible to overcome in action because of smoke, confusion and limited signalling facilities. But in doing this the instructions inevitably laid stress upon the line-ahead formation, and in the course of time the maintenance of the line itself became an end in its own right rather than the (rather unsatisfactory) means of fighting.

After 1744, when the British Admiralty issued 'The Permanent Fighting Instructions', the line had become absolutely sacrosanct. Yet, as has been pointed out by Professor Michael Lewis, in fifteen engagements between 1692 and 1782 when the British strictly adhered to the line, not one enemy ship was taken, and all these actions, obviously, ended

23

indecisively. Yet in those same years the British won six overwhelming victories amid the tumult and confusion of the general chase when British ships broke station to engage opportunity targets in the course of a pursuit of an enemy 'on the run'. This discrepancy between results was startling, but evidently natural caution, conservativism and the desire to preserve the established chain of command combined to ensure that the line, despite its inadequacies, remained for most of the century an article of tactical faith in the British Navy.

The line tactic thus had a paralysing effect on initiative until Rodney won an overwhelming victory at the Battle of the Saints in 1782. The success was not enough to prevent the loss of the American colonies, but it was enough to minimise losses elsewhere, and it shattered the hold of 'The Permanent Fighting Instructions'. Rodney, as much by accident as by design, broke his own line in order to break the French line in two places as his fleet and that of the French passed one another on opposite tracks, the French being to windward. What should have been a totally frustrating experience for the British turned out to be an overwhelming victory, mainly because a fortuitous change in the wind caused the French centre and rear to lose station with their sails against their masts. The French lost ten ships, flagship included, when the British enveloped their centre and rear. Similarly at Camperdown (1797) and Trafalgar first Duncan and then Nelson broke the enemy line in two places, thereby bringing an annihilating superiority of force against part of the enemy in both cases. But Duncan and Nelson deliberately planned to break the enemy line whereas Rodney improvised. At Camperdown the Dutch lost nine of their sixteen line-of-battle ships, while at Trafalgar the French and Spanish lost seventeen with only eleven making their way back to the safety of Cadiz.

Trafalgar is, of course, the acme of naval warfare under sail, but though much has been written about this battle perhaps it serves best as an illustration of the ability of these wooden ships to absorb punishment. Indeed it is hard to find a better example of their durability than the fight of the *Redoutable*. This French 74 was completely overshadowed by the ship directly in the line ahead of her, the 136-gun *Santissima Trinidada,* but it took three British battleships, including the 100-gun *Victory,* to reduce her after an action that cost the French ship 522 of her crew of 590. It was in the course of this fight that one of the marksmen on the *Redoutable* mortally wounded Nelson.

One of the unfortunate aspects of history, particularly of the popular kind, is its inevitable concentration on battle as the decisive element in the unfolding of events. The naval side of the Seven Years War (1756-1763) is told in terms of Byng's failure at Minorca that cost him his life, Lagos and Quiberon Bay, just as the naval history of the French Revolutionary and Napoleonic Wars (1793-1815) is narrated by the episodes of the Glorious First of June, Cape St Vincent, Camperdown, the Nile, Copenhagen and Trafalgar. Likewise, in more modern times, the story of the Pacific war (1941-1945) is invariably hung on Pearl Harbor, the Coral Sea, Midway, the Philippine Sea and Leyte Gulf.

Fleet engagements are obviously the most immediate and important element of naval warfare, given the fact that a won battle represents the most effective means of controlling an enemy's movements by sea. But in the Age of Sail, granted the generally indecisive nature of most sea fights, strategic deployment of force and the relative strength of the combatants were normally more potent factors in the deciding of the outcome of war at sea than battle itself. Even after Trafalgar, perhaps up until that time the most crushing and momentous sea battle for three hundred years, the British fleet was condemned to a decade-long vigil along the coasts of Europe to counter the movements of other enemy forces. The blockade of enemy ports was designed to ensure that the enemy made no move without being challenged, but in fact the victory at Trafalgar did not give the British anything they did not enjoy before battle. They already enjoyed command of the sea, and this meant that the British could use the sea for their own commercial and military purposes and could deny the same facilities to their enemies.

But a blockade and command of the seas can seldom, if ever, be total, and none of the blockades the British imposed on their enemies was ever fully successful in preventing enemy ships slipping in and out of port. With the choice of when and how to slip past a blockade, all the immediate advantages lay with the blockaded rather than the blockader. These simple facts, when combined with secure bases from which to mount blockade-running attempts and the continued existence of a 'fleet-in-being' to tie down British ships and prevent their use elsewhere, lay at the heart of the strategy usually employed by France in her wars with Britain - the *guerre de course,* commerce-destruction.

For France the guerre de course was an extremely attractive strategy, combining as it did few risks and little expenditure with the realistic hope of major profit. The guerre de course involved either royal ships or private ships (commissioned by a letter of marque to distinguish the 'privateer' from the 'pirate') carrying out 'cruising warfare' - attacks on enemy merchantmen by fast, light but heavily armed ships, the aim of such attacks being to capture merchantmen and bring them to friendly ports. It is perhaps surprising to talk of British command of the sea in successive wars between 1702 and 1815 and then to set out the huge totals of British merchantmen taken by Britain's enemies. In the first five years of the War of Spanish Succession (1702-1713) the British lost 1,416 merchantmen, but recaptured 300 of them, and in 1761 alone, at a time when Britain was unchallenged by a French Navy that did not put a single ship of the line to sea in the whole of the year, the British lost 812 ships. The latter figure represents about 10 per cent of all British merchantmen of all types in service at that time.

French losses, though numerically much smaller, were proportionately much greater. Heavy though British losses were, they could be absorbed, even if individuals and companies were bankrupted as a result. The simple truth of the guerre de course was, as the great American naval historian Mahan noted in *The Influence of Sea Power upon History, 1660-1783,* that: 'such a war . . . cannot stand alone . . . Failing . . . support, the cruiser can only dash out hurriedly a short distance from home, and its blows, though painful, cannot be fatal . . . worrying, but not deadly.'

Mahan, in his comments on the War of 1812, noted the success of American frigates and privateers, but was equally alive to the fact that when the British brought the full weight of their forces to bear they enjoyed such success, including the burning of Washington, that: 'When negotiations for peace were opened, the bearing of the English (*sic*) towards the American envoys was not that of men who felt their country to be threatened with an unbearable evil.'

In effect Mahan pointed out that a strategy of commerce destruction was certain to be attritional and slow to take its toll. It never really had genuine hopes of inflicting permanent and significant damage on a nation that possessed command of the sea and could not be a substitute for command. As one British observer noted at the time, the remarkable thing about the 1761 losses was not that they were so heavy but that they were not even greater. Command of the sea kept losses down to a point where they were tolerable.

With the exception of Navarino (1827) Trafalgar was the last major battle fought between sailing ships. The American Revolution and the French Revolution were followed by the British Revolution, or as it is more often called, the Industrial Revolution. This was to lead to the eruption of British power in particular, and European power in general, throughout the world in the course of the nineteenth century. In the era of the sailing ship western technology was only marginally superior to that of China and Japan though much superior to that of the rest of the world. Had it not been for the desire of China and Japan to exclude themselves from the rest of the world in order to preserve their social structures, the process of colonialisation may well have been an eastern and not a western phenomenon. But the Industrial Revolution took place in the west, and it led to a scientific, technological and material advancement in Europe that was to result in the rest of the world, the USA excluded, languishing behind for many generations.

In naval terms what the Industrial Revolution did was to destroy the harmony and symmetry of naval engineering that had evolved over the previous four centuries. The man-of-war of Nelson's day was incapable of further qualitative improvement. It had developed to the point where its effectiveness was to slip into obsolescence as new and better material became available. The 'new and superior' related to one thing - power, and in the Industrial Revolution this meant steam.

In naval terms the coming of the steam engine restored movement independent of sea and wind. This had been lost when the galley and galeass gave way to sail. To escape from doldrums, to leave harbour against contrary headwinds and to bestow tactical mobility on a line in battle were all obvious advantages to be gained from incorporating steam at sea, but inevitably engines had their drawbacks. They needed coal, and this meant that the first price steam exacted was the loss of endurance: steam meant a reversion to 'short haul' navies. Moreover, engines needed space, and this could only be made available by a reduction of offensive power. The first steam engines at sea turned paddle wheels, and these had to be carried high (and were thus vulnerable to gunfire) making great inroads into the number of cannon that could be carried in broadside. The first steam engines were more of a liability than an asset to navies, not least because of their dubious reliability. Until the development of the propeller as the means of propulsion which allowed engines to be carried deep into the bowels of a ship, the steam engine had very little impact on naval architecture.

The first steam-powered warship was proposed, and launched, by the Americans in response to their worsening strategic situation at British hands in the War of 1812. The *Demologos* was a twin-hulled floating battery with her paddle wheels carried internally. She was conceived as the means of attacking the British squadrons blockading New York and was not a real warship capable of operating on the open sea. But with the end of that war and that of the Napoleonic wars in Europe, the first attempts to incorporate steam power in naval vessels came to an end. Steam, when it was introduced into navies, came in a much humbler form of ship - tugs that were used to take sailing ships to sea against the wind. In the 'twenties the British Navy built three such tugs, the *Monkey* of 1821 being the first to enter service. But developments in the merchant service, and in particular the appearance of Brunel's steamship *Great Britain*, could not be ignored by admiralties. The *Great Britain* was a remarkable ship by any standard. She was the largest ship in the world at the time of her launch and she was the first ocean-going ship to be built in iron. She incorporated a clipper bow, a balanced rudder and screw propulsion, and her construction prompted the British Admiralty in 1845 to propose building warships in iron in future. Such was the public outcry at this proposal that the admiralty recanted, but in the end such a move was inevitable if for no other reason than Europe was quickly exhausting its supplies of seasoned oak.

By the mid-1850s, however, the screw was being fitted to an increasing number of warships as a means of auxiliary power, the French leading the British in this process. But advances in the chemical and metallurgical fields were also in hand and from mid-century onwards began to intrude on naval calculations. Solid cannon balls were an inefficient method of destruction. At point-blank range a 32-lb shot could smash its way through 18-in of oak, but of course it could not explode within a ship and, as we have seen, it was very difficult to pound a warship into destruction. But in 1841 a Frenchman, Colonel Paixhans, invented a new type of explosive shell that was designed to explode after it had penetrated the side of a ship. It became obvious to munitions firms in many countries that a cylindrical shell, particularly when fired from a rifled barrel, had far superior ballistic properties and powers of penetration than shot. When this realisation was married to the development of new chemicals both as propellant and explosive charge, it was evident that offensive power was on the point of advance for the first time since the introduction of cannon itself.

The development of shells obviously posed an alarming threat to sailing ships which, being made of wood, were hopelessly vulnerable to flame. A few rounds of Paixhans-type shells were certain to have a more deadly effect than successive broadsides of shot, and this became very evident from the one and only battle fought with shells during the Age of Sail. At the Battle of Sinope in November 1853 the Russian Black Sea Fleet had shells and the Turks did not, with very predictable results. But the same technology that was providing shells produced a counter to them - armour. It was a simple expedient to fasten iron plates on wooden hulls to counter the effect of shells, as the French showed in the course of the Crimean War (1854-1856) when the Russians tried to repeat their Sinope success against Anglo-French warships. French protected warships proved invulnerable to Russian shells. The French move was only an expedient, but the long-term implication was obvious. Ships had to be purpose-built to withstand shell-fire, and this could only mean the end of wood as the material in which ships were built. Wood was too vulnerable to flame, but equally important was the fact that steam engines, new and heavier guns and the demands of armour protection were adding weights beyond the strength of wooden frames, and this could only mean that ships would have to be built in metal in future. In 1858 the French hesitatingly grasped this nettle. In that year they laid down a frigate at Toulon. *La Gloire* was an iron-protected warship but she had a wooden hull. She was, however, the first of a programme of four frigates and with the fourth the French proposed to build a ship entirely of iron. The French, however, were forestalled by the British who in December 1860 launched the world's first iron warship, the *Warrior*. With this ship a new era of naval construction was to dawn.

The *Warrior* ushered in a period of almost constant material change that was to last into the first decade of the present century. In essence this period of change centred around the struggle between the artillery manufacturer and the steel maker for the upper hand as heavier and more powerful guns became available but ever thicker and improved armour was added to ships in an effort to ensure that they had reasonable chances of surviving combat with their equals.

The problem that surrounded these developments was that men were working to the limits of existing scientific knowledge and had no pool of information and experience on which to draw as they designed, armed and protected successive generations of warships. The old symmetry disappeared as nations went their own ways though by the turn of the century designs has basically stabilised and a rough similarity of design had reimposed itself on all nations. In the meantime, however, results were varied to say the least. Not a few ships that were built might well have entered a competition to determine the least seaworthy ship ever constructed.

The British *Captain* was such a ship, and she was lost during a gale in September 1870 for the very simple reason that she combined the worst possible blend of old and new. She carried both sail and steam, but her masts were the tallest and heaviest in the Royal Navy. She had a greater proportional length to beam (just over 6:1) than any major warship built to date, and she had two decks. On the lower deck, designed to be just 8.5-ft above the water line, she carried four 12-in guns in two turrets, but her freeboard was reduced during construction as extra weight was worked into her. The combination of low centre of gravity and top-heavy masts caused her to founder in a storm she should have survived. Her loss substantially helped the suppression of masts and rigging. Only three battleships after the *Captain* carried a full rig, and steam thereafter emerged as the only means of propulsion used in British warships.

The loss of the *Captain* also resulted in the suppression of the turret. This, however, proved only temporary because the need to place all guns and their crews behind armour protection came to be regarded as essential. The process in fact had begun with *La Gloire,* but not the *Warrior,* and the French followed this by placing all the guns of the *Magenta* and *Solferino,* the only two-decked broadside ironclads ever built, within an armoured citadel.

But since guns and armour cancelled one another out, the *Warrior* and *La Gloire* represented no relative advance over wooden men-of-war. Their armour made them all but invulnerable to gunfire, and hence reduced their own offensive power. They could absorb punishment but could not inflict decisive damage on ships similarly protected - as the *Monitor* and *Merrimac* proved in their historic encounter in March 1862. To overcome armour, therefore, guns became heavier, and this resulted in the removal of the broadside in favour of fewer but more powerful and destructive guns. Initially such guns were pivotal and were moved along arcs that allowed them to train through restricted arcs of fire via gun ports made in the citadel. This was the arrangement incorporated in the first turrets. The armoured housing itself remained stationary while the gun was moved on a turntable and fired through fixed ports. It was inevitable, however, that with fewer guns the need for all-round fire should prevail, and this could only mean the turret as a whole should revolve. For a time open barbettes - guns with no housing - were favoured, but gradually the turret became incorporated as a standard feature of heavy armament carried on warships.

For a time, guns became not so much heavy as monstrous as better protection forced all navies to increase their size. The Italian battleship *Duilio,* for example, was laid down in 1872 and it was planned that she should carry four 12-in 38-ton guns. But during construction she was modified to take first 15-in 50-ton guns and finally 17.7-in 100-ton guns. Her final appearance was widely acclaimed, even though she had virtually no armour. The British response included the *Inflexible* with 80-ton muzzle loaders that had to be depressed in order to reload. She also carried 24-in of compound armour (iron backed by teak and steel) over her vital parts and 22-in bulkheads. She also incorporated an armoured deck below the water line and was extensively sub-divided in order to facilitate damage control.

The era of the very heavy gun was short-lived, lasting not much more than a decade or so. No sooner had its praises been extolled than its weaknesses began to be appreciated. Awesome though their destructive powers might be reckoned to be, such guns were extremely slow to fire, wildly inaccurate and had blast effects that prevented echeloned guns firing together. The *Inflexible,* with one round every two minutes, was by the standards of the day a fast firer, but against a fast-moving enemy even she had little chance of registering hits. At a gunnery trial in 1871 the single 12-in gun of the *Hotspur,* carried in one of those fixed turrets, contrived to miss the target at 200 yards, both the *Hotspur* and target being stationary in a flat calm. The blast effects of such guns, moreover, always threatened to do far more damage to the user than their shells could visit upon an enemy. Ships simply could not take the strain imposed by the prolonged firing of their own weapons.

The solution to these problems was at hand, however, in the form of new weapons and steel. Towards the end of the nineteenth century, as the negative aspects of sulphur and the positive aspects of phosphorous in steel making became increasingly appreciated, steel ceased to be a very expensive and comparatively rare material and became widely used. Similarly guns at last freed themselves from old muzzle loading concepts. The first breech-loaders had had many weaknesses, those of the *Warrior,* for example, being suppressed because they were inferior to the muzzle-loaders. But by the last two decades or so of the nineteenth century the manufacturers had perfected means of sealing the breech effectively, thus increasing the power of the gun, and they were now capable of making much lighter guns with far higher rates of fire. The quick-firing gun appeared for the first time on a British warship with the *Nile* and *Trafalgar,* laid down in 1886, and by that time ships were beginning to appear that were recognisable as the forerunners of gunned surface ships in the first half of the present century. The race between guns and armour had nowhere near run its course, but by the last two decades of the nineteenth century battleships carried a heavy main armament fore and aft and grouped secondary and tertiary armament in batteries amidship around the command posts and funnels. The relative lightness of guns and armour restored high freeboard, making ships faster, drier and more seaworthy.

But the great advantage of these new arrangements lay in the fact that in the place of a few very heavy rounds a battleship could now fire a considerable volume of assorted ordnance very quickly. It was generally held that many hits, even with the lightest shells, were more important than a few hits even by the heaviest of rounds. The reasoning behind this was that an enemy would be demoralised and damaged by smothering fire and this would allow ranges to be closed and the enemy destroyed by more deliberate fire. This was the lesson drawn by some commentators from the Battle of Tsushima in May 1905 when the Japanese fleet routed the Russian Baltic Fleet as it tried to force its way to Vladivostok via the strait between Korea and Japan. This conclusion was based on a count of guns available to both sides. The Russian preponderance in heavy guns failed to save them from decisive defeat, and Japanese superiority in medium and heavy artillery was deemed to have been the decisive factor in their success. Such a view reflected the then current obsession with matériel and failed to take proper account of the yawning disparity between the two sides in terms of morale, discipline, training, command, tactical ability and quality of equipment.

The truth of Tsushima was that the Russian Baltic Fleet was no more than an ill-assorted rabble with a commander who failed to command. After ordering his fleet into line ahead formation Admiral Rozhestvensky did not issue another order during a battle that quickly turned into a massacre. The Japanese, under Togo, quickly realised the poor quality of the opposition and closed in to administer the coup de grâce after having first carried out the classic tactic of crossing the enemy T. This involved deploying the battle line in file across the line of the enemy's advance. With all its guns unmasked the fleet crossing the T was then able to bring concentrated fire against an enemy line unable to reply in kind because it could only respond with its forward guns and some of those would have their fields of fire masked by the ships further up the line. Only after this initial exchange - when the Russians in fact shot well but unluckily - did the Japanese, having already inflicted considerable damage on Rozhestvensky's fleet, turn and close the range and thus bring about the annihilation of the Russian force. It was obvious from Togo's handling of his fleet that he had a clear disdain for Russian capabilities.

There was, however, another interpretation of Tsushima, and this was that the differences between the two sides were so great that no material or tactical conclusions could be drawn from the battle with any safety. Such a view tended to discount the Japanese closing of the range and laid far greater emphasis on other events in the war and in the very first stages of the battle itself. The ease with which Togo outmanoeuvred Rozhestvensky was attributed as much to the Russian's ineptitude as the fact that Japanese ships possessed a clear superiority of speed over Russian warships, and there was no getting away from the fact that a superiority in speed gave immense tactical advantages, other things being equal. Earlier battles between Russian and Japanese warships also served as pointers to the future. In the battle off Port Arthur on 10 August 1904 the Russians had overshot the Japanese line at 10-miles range and had inflicted what could easily have proved crippling damage on Togo's flagship, the *Mikasa,* at 13,000 yards. Even at Tsushima fire had been opened at 7,000 yards, at least 2,000 yards beyond the practice ranges of most navies at that time. Ranges were increasing because of technical developments in other fields. These concerned the torpedo and its gradual but significant improvements in speed, range, size of warhead and reliability. By about 1905 the torpedo had acquired a maximum range of about 4,000 yards or a high speed run at about 33 knots to about 1,000 yards. It was evident, therefore, that future battle ranges would have to open. There could be no repeat of such battles as that of Manila Bay during the Spanish-American war of 1898 when battle ranges had been about 250 yards.

But even at Manila Bay the two forces had achieved less than 3 per cent hits, and the Spanish line had been at anchor because its ships were too unseaworthy to leave the protection of the bay. If ranges opened, therefore, immediate problems of gunnery control and accuracy emerged. In part the answer was provided by a British admiral, Scott, who in the first decade of the century invented a satisfactory ranging device and a sub-calibre training instrument that resulted in a drastic improvement in British gunnery. But Scott and other thoughtful gunnery officers in various navies considered the value of medium and light artillery dubious at the unprecedented range of 7,000 yards and above. They believed that only the heaviest guns seemed likely to inflict significant damage on a competently manned battleship. Moreover, with a variety of guns it was impossible to spot individual fire at long ranges. Without centralised control and with differential times of flight for different calibres to a given range, it was impossible to aim and control fire effectively. If ranges were to open uniformity of gun size was essential because this alone allowed uniform time of flight for salvo firing, range being corrected after observers had noted the fall of shot relative to the enemy.

Such was the logic behind the British construction of the *Dreadnought,* the first all-big gun battleship in the world, completed in 1906. This ship was the father of all subsequent battleships built after that date because all nations followed the British lead along a path that led them within 35 years from the ten 12-in guns of the 17,900-ton 'prototype' to the graceful magnificence of the 72,000 tons of Japan's *Yamato* and *Musashi* with their main armament of nine 18.1-in. guns.

But a four-fold increase in size and a change from 800-lb shells that could fire 12,000 yards to 3,000-lb shells that could be fired 27 miles was paralleled by the battleship's declining effectiveness. The *Yamato* and *Musashi* were like the galeass in comparison to the sailing ship. The galeass represented the final form of a weapons system that was passing into obsolescence because of the development of technology. This was the case with the Japanese super-battleships. As some Japanese commanders argued even at the time when the *Yamato* was laid down, she was obsolete, rendered thus by developments in naval aviation.

The story of battleship evolution between the *Dreadnought* and

Yamato was one of constant endeavours to maintain the effectiveness of such ships in the face of the challenge posed by torpedo and bomb. It was, in the end, a struggle that was lost, and in the losing of it the battleship ceased to be the arbiter of naval warfare, a position that it had enjoyed, in some shape or form, since the dawn of naval warfare. In these three or so decades that separated the *Dreadnought* from the greatest battleships ever built navies lavished massive efforts into improving the defences (passive and active) and the offensive power of their gunned capital ships. As a result the battleships built in the interwar period and during the Second World War were far better prepared than their First World War forebears to fight for and secure command of the sea, had not submarines and aircraft changed the nature of naval warfare.

The First World War proved to be the last war when the battleship proved to be the main instrument of sea power, but such was the pressure being exerted on its traditional supremacy by the submarine that in that war there was a stalemate at sea just as surely as there was a more obvious stalemate on land. Britain, through her geographical position and superiority of numbers, commanded the sea or rather the surface of the sea, with certain exceptions - such as the Black and Baltic Seas. But this command was countered by German superiority in submarine warfare which, after a few false starts, pursued a guerre de course. Germany narrowly but decisively failed to win this war against British, allied and neutral shipping, and this allowed the strategic aspects of sea power to play a decisive part in deciding the outcome of the war.

This was the case because, with a decisive result proving elusive on land between August 1914 and July 1918, the economic aspects of sea power became increasingly important in the conduct of war. In simple terms, though the impact of sea power on national economies had been lessened by the development of fast, cheap and safe methods of overland communications, the development of a global economy and the increasing sophistication of industry that depended on imported raw materials resulted in naval blockade retaining its potency. Britain's geographical position, across German lines of communication with the outside world, enabled her gradually but remorselessly to strangle the life out of Germany and her allies. German success in the east came too late to offset the creeping paralysis that affected German industry and agriculture, and in the end, when the realisation of Germany's failure during the Victory Offensive of the spring and summer of 1918 beganto percolate through to the German civil population, it was the dread of having to face another winter at war that was instrumental in breaking German military and civil morale in the autumn of 1918.

There was good reason for such despair for in the course of the war at least 800,000 people died in Germany from starvation and many more succumbed to diseases attributable in whole or in part to malnutrition or vitamin deficiency caused by the blockade. By 1918 German cereal production was 40 per cent down on its 1913 level, potato production had been halved and suger beet yields had fallen by a third, largely as a result of lack of fertilisers caused by the cutting off of imports. All forms of drugs and even bandages were in desperately short supply by 1918 and German industry could not make good the deficiencies caused by an economic blockade that covered 338 items, excluding by-products and derivatives, by the summer of 1918. German industrial production declined by 40 per cent in the course of the war, and at the war's end Germany was industrially, financially and physically at the end of her tether. The main reason for this was the allied application of sea power. The blockade was unglamorous, but it was insidious and devastatingly effective.

The British blockade was different from the counter-blockade German submarines tried to impose on Britain in one vital respect. It did not sink merchantmen, and in particular it did not sink neutral (pre-April 1917) American merchantmen. The British blockade, however, was not just a naval affair: the emergence of total war ensured that the naval aspects of blockade had to be supplemented by the use of other non-military aspects of power. These included the use of diplomatic and financial power to ensure that the Germans were denied materials in neutral countries and that the neutral states in Europe - such as The Netherlands and the Scandanavian countries - did not provide the Germans with goods they would otherwise be denied. The neutrals were more or less 'rationed' to their pre-war import levels by the British, and in order to forestall trouble with the Americans the British at various times bought their cotton crop, stockpiles of raw materials and even individual ship cargoes at over market rates simply in order to deny the Germans the chance to buy them and then enbroil the British in a dispute with the Americans over 'Freedom of navigation'. The blockade itself, on the military side, was imposed by mines and patrolling the waters that washed the British Isles. Warships and armed merchant cruisers patrolled waters through which merchant ships would have to pass in an effort to reach Germany, but the backbone of the blockade was the British Grand Fleet. From its base at Scapa Flow the Grand Fleet controlled all German naval movements except in the Baltic. Geography dictated that when war came the German High Sea Fleet could do nothing to prevent or raise this blockade.

In this situation the British had only to avoid defeat to retain their

35

command of the sea, and victory in battle was not essential to them in strategic terms, though victory would produce certain not insubstantial military advantages and immense political dividends. The Germans, on the other hand, could not hope to secure any permanent advantage even from a successful action. German ships could not break out into the Atlantic because there was no place for them to go except back home. But defeat had to be avoided by the High Seas Fleet. Without the support of a fleet-in-being British minelayers would have been able to mine ever closer to the German coast, ultimately confining German submarines to their ports. British minesweepers would have been able to deal with German minefields, thereby exposing German territory to the possibility of amphibious attack, while the defeat of German capital ships would have allowed their British counterparts, with their cruisers and escorts, to have been switched to other duties and theatres. Moreover, the continued existence of an undefeated German fleet was immensely important politically and diplomatically and gave the Germans some lever against the British in dealings with neutrals.

Thus the Germans were always reluctant to join battle, even though they knew that a victory would be an important morale-booster for a nation that felt itself increasingly isolated and embattled. The German fleet was too valuable to be risked in any marginal enterprise, but the Germans persistently hoped to catch a large detached part of the Grand Fleet - not too large a part - and administer on it a severe local defeat. Such a victory formed part of Germany's attritional strategy at sea - the wearing down of British numerical superiority to the point where a general engagement might be fought with reasonable hope of success. The British, however, were very wary of leaving weak detachments unsupported and they turned their faces away from the prospect of venturing too far into the southern North Sea for fear of German mines and patrol lines of submarines.

With the Germans reluctant to advance very far to the north for fear of being caught by a superior British force it is hardly surprising that the only fleet action in the North Sea during the whole of the First World War, the Battle of Jutland of 31 May-1 June 1916, came about as a result of an accident. Neither side knew that the other was out in strength, the British because of faulty intelligence interpretation, the Germans out of ignorance, and with the single important exception of British light cruisers during the preliminary skirmishes, both sides were very badly served by their reconnaissance forces. Both fleet commanders, Jellicoe for the British and Sheer for the Germans, fought the battle almost blind since in those days there were no radars to aid tracking, gunnery and deployment. Both sides sought to engage in line ahead formation and to join action with broadside fire, but the lack of knowledge of enemy strengths and positions, the lack of quick and reliable communications between ships and a total absence of tactical flexibility conspired to produce an indecisive result. In so many ways Jutland represented no real advance over one of the many indecisive battles in the Age of Sail. The rigidity of 'The Permanent Fighting Instructions' was directly paralleled by 'The Grand Fleet Battle Orders', while the ability to command once in action had shown no major improvement over the previous hundred years because non-visual methods of communication had not improved at the same pace as other aspects of matériel.

Nevertheless, in the course of the battle basic skills of seamanship were high and certain aspects of tactical handling by both commanders was of a superb standard. The passing of sail had not lessened the importance of wind, sea and light: the weather gage, albeit in modified form, still existed. Wind was a vital consideration in that the line nearest the wind had its funnel and gun smoke cleared into the sea between the lines while the line to leeward was left unmasked. At the Battle of the Falklands in December 1914 the British temporarily ceased fire while they manoeuvred for the windward position, and at Jutland the same consideration was equally important. Light was even more important. In long ranged exchanges to catch an enemy against a weak sun whilst remaining undetectable against a black background was vital. At Coronel in November 1914 a German squadron had annihilated a weak British force by using this tactic, and in another war British light cruisers were to repeat the tactic against the *Graf Spee* during the Battle of the River Plate in December 1939. At Jutland Jellicoe successfully manoeuvred for the better light, and by the same manoeuvre he not only placed his fleet in a position to cross the German T as Sheer came north but also brought his force around the German flank and hence was in a position to place the British fleet between the Germans and their base. Jellicoe's deployment of his fleet in this manner, at a time when he did not fully know the whereabouts of the German line, is rightly ranked amongst the greatest manoeuvres in naval history, but even this could not forestall the German master card, the simultaneous battle turn away through 180°. The Germans had practised this turning of their ships together in order to get themselves out of just this kind of situation. At Jutland they twice used the *gefechtskehrtwendung* to extricate themselves from positions that they should never have placed themselves in to start with, and during the hours of darkness they fought their way back to the safety of the home-side position through the rear of the British fleet. In night fighting the Germans proved vastly superior to the British who had badly neglected this aspect of warfare. British passivity during the night and their failure to react to the battle taking place at the rear of their line was one of the major British failures of the engagement.

Jutland was an intense disappointment for the British, largely because impossible expectations on the part of the public demanded annihilating victory in the best traditions of the Royal Navy. The balance of losses strongly favoured the Germans. But as an American newspaper commented at the time, the prisoner had assaulted the warden, but was still in prison, and the simple truth of the situation was that battles are decided by results, not losses. British losses could be absorbed; those of the Germans less so. Yet the real point was that British command of the sea had not been affected one iota by the battle. For all her claims of victory Germany did not improve her strategic position in any way as a result of Jutland, though the British failure to destroy the High Seas Fleet naturally diminished the status of the Royal Navy throughout the world. Never again did the Royal Navy possess its traditional moral superiority over every other navy because the battle had shown many unsatisfactory aspects of British naval preparations. British signalling, fire distribution and accuracy of gunnery in the initial exchanges between the heavy reconnaissance forces were poor, while the Germans had proved better than the British in finding battle ranges quickly. The Germans used the simple technique of quick salvo firing and correcting fire thereafter: the more deliberate British spotted individual salvoes and then corrected. The British could hold ranges better than the Germans, but the German technique allowed them to make the first hits, and these proved fatal to three British capital ships. But even allowing for these deficiencies of technique, the crucial point about the battle was that the British and not the Germans had been strategically correct in their assessment. The Germans had not thought naval policy through to the point beyond battle: battle was an end in itself. The British saw battle as the means to an end, and in this they were quite correct - and victorious in the strategic sense, if not tactically.

In the fields of tactics and technology the battle showed that the then-existing command and fire-control arrangements were inadequate. The advances in destructive power over the previous generations had not been paralleled by improvements in command and tactics that would have maximised the effectiveness of the new firepower. Indeed, in fire-control the Admiralty failed to make use of the best existing technology: the Pollen system. For both signalling and range-correction battle fleets were dependent on the human eyeball which could not resolve the problems caused by heavy funnel and gun smoke, smoke screens, poor natural light and the restriction of vision on board a fast-moving warship. All these problems were to be remedied (to a greater or lesser extent) during the inter-war period and by the Second World War most had been overcome by the introduction of radar and aircraft to scout and correct gunfire. But straight artillery duels between heavy ships in the 1939-1945 conflict were few. In the European war only one capital ship, the *Hood,* was sunk in a fire fight, and though in the Pacific the Americans enjoyed two most notable successes in gunnery engagements - off Guadal canal in November 1942 when the *Washington* and *South Dakota* accounted for the *Kirishima* and later in October 1944 when their battle line hammered a Japanese force in the Surigao Strait during the Leyte Gulf engagement - these were very much the exceptions. The battleship's role had become restricted to a subordinate, secondary one in support of carriers. Battleships played extremely important roles in convoy protection, shore-bombardment and the movement of personnel and treasure, but their prime role (particularly in the Pacific) was to provide cover for carriers against surface ship and aircraft attack. In fact on the only two occasions when battleships were needed to defend carriers against surface attack, they were absent, the British losing the *Glorious* and the Americans the *Gambier Bay* on these separate occasions. But against enemy air attack battleships proved on many occasions to be invaluable support for carriers. With their massed banks of AA guns the battleship gave carriers a support that the latter could not provide for themselves because of their clear flight decks. The Korean and Vietnamese Wars were to show that even after the Second World War naval guns still had a vital role to play in enforcing blockade and in supporting land forces, but only if air supremacy already existed. Naval superiority and command of the sea were phenomena no longer synonymous with battleships and their escorts in the era after sea warfare had become three dimensional - on, above and below the surface of the sea.

CHAPTER III

HIDDEN FROM VIEW:
THE SUBMARINE AND THE MINE

The desire to strike an enemy ship at its most vulnerable point, on or below the waterline, exercised a fascination on military and scientific minds throughout the Age of Sail. The passing of the galley and galeass and their replacement by gunned sailing ships that could not, unlike their predecessors, ram an enemy in no way seems to have dampened enthusiasm and experimentation in the search for new methods of underwater attack. The simple fact of the matter was, however, that until wood ceased to be the basic material for ships, and until a new form of reliable and safe propulsion emerged, the search for an underwater weapon was certain to be unsuccessful. When these various elements materialised, of course, not only did underwater attack become possible, but the sailing ship itself had been superseded.

Before studying this development it is as well to deal with and then dismiss from further consideration the reappearance of the ram in the course of the second half of the nineteenth century. The restoration of the power of independent movement, earlier sacrificed to meet the demands of the cannon for its own platform, naturally created the essential pre-condition for the return of the ram, and after the sinking of the Italian battleship *Re d'Italia* which was rammed by the Austrian battleship *Ferdinand Max* at the Battle of Lissa in 1866, the ram became a vogue weapon. It was widely felt at the time that the ram was likely to prove, once again, the decisive weapon at sea, and for a brief time rambattleships, heavily armoured in the bows with heavy artillery concentrated forward in the manner favoured by Don Juan at Lepanto, were built by many navies. Such a development flew in the face of all the evidence available even at the time. That many rammings were attempted at Lissa and only one was successful went unnoticed or was ignored, as did the very obvious fact that previous to her being rammed the *Re d'Italia* had been crippled by gunfire. Ramming was increasingly unrealistic as speeds rose (presuming ships had sea room in which to manoeuvre) and the development of fire power was certain to diminish the prospect of successfully closing the range to a point where ramming was possible. Ramming at best was a hazardous expedient since it always threatened to do as much damage to the attacker as the intended victim, but there was no denying the fact that even well-built battleships could ram one another to destruction. Sir George Tryon inadvertently proved this when in 1893 he contrived to lose his own flagship, the *Victoria,* to the bows of the *Camperdown* in the course of a dubious manoeuvre that went awry. By the time that the *Dreadnought* appeared to herald the further opening of ranges and even higher speeds the ram on capital ships was obsolete, but right up until the First World War ram bows were incorporated into battleship design. Perversely, probably the last battleship to ram an enemy in action was the *Dreadnought* herself when in 1915 she ran down U-9, a German submarine.

Of course it was the submarine, as we have noted elsewhere, that posed the main threat to the surface ship's supremacy during the First World War, but it was not the only or even the first of the underwater challenges that began to restrict the ability of surface ships to operate in any stretch of water except those immediately covered by shore positions. The submarine, however, was not a weapon but a weapons platform and it was not, before the advent of nuclear propulsion, strictly speaking a submarine at all. It was a surface ship that had the ability to submerge and travel underwater at low speed and for a limited duration.

The submarine's main weapon was the torpedo, but it was not until the latter part of the nineteenth century that the word 'torpedo' came to denote a self-propelled explosive charge that ran on or near the surface of the sea. When Farragut at Mobile Bay in 1864 made his 'Damn the torpedoes, full speed ahead,' comment that has passed into US Navy folklore, he actually meant Confederate mines since at that time 'torpedo' was an all-embracing word used to describe any type of underwater weapon, and in fact the torpedo in its present context had still to be invented.

Mines were not given the power of movement for the very good reason that their value lay in being deliberately and permanently sited in certain locations, and as a result they were moored to the seabed. An American, Robert Fulton, is generally credited with the invention of the mine in the late eighteenth century when he packed an explosive mixture into a sealed container and used a clockwork mechanism to set off the charge. The drawback of this device was the obvious one of a lack of deliberate initiation: activation by clockwork was too random to be effective. Some method of controlled initiation was needed to make a mine explode when in contact with the target, and the first solution to this need was provided by another American, Samuel Colt, the inventor of the revolver.

Colt devised a controlled mine that was activated by an electrical charge from an observation post ashore. In Germany the same technique was being developed at roughly the same time and electrically-controlled minefields were used for the first time in the defence of Kiel harbour against the possibility of an attack by the Danish fleet during the upheavals of 1848.

The electrically-controlled minefield came to play an extremely important role in providing passive defence for fleet bases. Because it was controlled by an operator ashore, friendly ships could pass over such a minefield in safety, but an enemy, particularly an enemy submarine that would otherwise be undetectable, would have its presence betrayed by indicator loops installed on the seabed. These generated a series of electrical currents whose magnetic fields were affected when the circuits were crossed by a vessel. When such interference was registered and a visual check revealed the absence of friendly forces the minefield could be detonated immediately and with an almost 100 per cent guarantee of destroying an intruder. At the very end of the First World War the British in this manner destroyed a German submarine that tried to enter the Scapa Flow base. What that submarine might have achieved was revealed by the success of U-47 when she entered Scapa in October 1939 and sank the *Royal Oak* at her moorings. The German submarine was able to make her way into the Flow because the anti-submarine defences of the base had not been completed and indicator loops were not in position.

Such minefields had certain weaknesses. They were relatively sophisticated and needed maintenance and crews to operate them. Moreover, they could only play a worthwhile role in certain restricted waters, such as harbour approaches. For an extended stretch of coast some other form of mine that was less demanding in capital and manpower outlay was needed, hence the attractiveness of contact mines. Such mines could only be set off when they were in collision with a ship - a strength and a weakness since the weapon remained in place unless actually struck but could not be 'influenced' to explode and could not differentiate between friend and enemy.

Contact mines were spheres with protruding horns. A blow from the bottom or the side of a passing ship would damage these horns, breaking phials containing an acid that reacted with a mixture of potassium chlorate and sugar. This produced an intense heat and flame sufficient to set out the main charge, and the shock effect of the explosion, being much greater through water than through air, was enough at least to damage the target. Though the actual components of initiation and charge varied from time to time because of improvements in chemicals

42

and explosives, the basic principle of using mechanical activation for the mine remained. Some contact mines operated when the action of being tilted over by a passing ship closed an electrical circuit.

The key to the mine's effectiveness was in the fact that it was normally concealed since it was laid to set depths and not left on the surface. A safe method of laying mines to a prescribed depth proved difficult to find until the British, who were usually very reticent about developing underwater weapons, solved the problem by devising a mine with a sinker or anchor that descended to the seabed. An automatic release mechanism freed the mine to rise on a cable from its sinker once the laying ship was clear. When the mine reached its required depth water-pressure activated a hydrostat which in turn operated a brake on the cable. Since the mine was already primed it was therefore ready for service.

These two basic types of mine, the electrically-controlled and the contact mine, were those that saw almost a monopoly of service in the period up to and including the First World War. The first major war that witnessed the use of mines was the Crimean War when the Russians used them extensively but without inflicting loss on the British and French fleets. The first victim of mines was the USS *Cairo* in the course of the Battle of the Yazoo River in 1862, but by the turn of the century the mine had developed into a formidable and dangerous weapon. In the course of the Russo-Japanese War, the first war when mines were extensively used by both sides, the Russians lost a battleship, a cruiser, two destroyers and two other warships and the Japanese lost two battleships (their only capital ship losses of the war), four cruisers, two destroyers, a torpedo boat and a minelayer to mines. Within three months of the outbreak of the First World War mines again showed their capabilities when a German mine accounted for one of Britain's latest and most powerful dreadnoughts, the *Audacious,* off the northern coast of Ireland.

The loss of the *Audacious* clearly pointed to the offensive use of the mine as a weapon of attrition that was designed to create a hazard to the movement of an enemy. This was the characteristic of Japanese mining activity during the Russo-Japanese war when the Japanese had mined as close to the Russian fleet base at Port Arthur as possible in order to contain the Russian squadrons to harbour and to inflict losses on them in the event of a sortie. Principally, however, the mine was a defensive weapon in that fields could be sown to protect coastlines from attack or to cover stretches of water through which trade could safely pass. In these roles mines offered every nation, even the least powerful, some measure of defence against even the most powerful. Mines were a means of gaining some measure of power (if only the negative power of denying for a time another nation free use of certain parts of the sea) on the cheap. The most powerful of warships were vulnerable to mines and a nation did not have to build battleships to sink an enemy injudicious enough to risk his forces in unsafe waters. This was precisely the way in which German mines carried out a strategic role in the course of the First World War. Their presence denied the British control of the southern North Sea, the mines and the High Seas Fleet providing one another with mutual protection and in doing so allowed the U-boats to continue to move in and out of their bases. But perhaps a better example of the defensive use of mines was the allied Dover Barrage laid during the war in the English Channel in order to deny egress through the Dover Strait. For much of the war the Dover Barrage was little more than an expensive sieve which had a conspicuous lack of success in preventing German submarines from making their way into a restricted area of sea where unprotected merchantmen abounded. It was only in the course of 1917-1918, and particularly the latter year, that the Barrage became properly organised, and only then did it manage to achieve its strategic objective - the denial of access to given waters on the part of the enemy. By a system of nets and mines, the latter being laid at various depths between 30 and 100-ft, and backed by surface ships that ranged from drifters to destroyers, the British forced an unacceptable rate of loss on German U-boats attempting to take the direct route into the Channel and North Atlantic.

To cut their losses the Germans were forced to send their submarines into the Atlantic via the seas to the north of Scotland. This may not seem to amount to very much, and certainly not to something of strategic significance. But the forcing of German submarines to take the northern route had immense strategic repercussions. It cut the time that German submarines could spend on patrol in the Atlantic by between ten and fourteen days, and increased the strain on crew and submarine alike. In simple terms the effectiveness of sea denial presented by the Dover Barrage reduced the operational effectiveness of German submarines in 1918 by perhaps as much as 30 per cent and this, combined with other factors, was decisive in ensuring that allied losses at sea did not force Germany's western enemies to sue for terms. This had seemed a distinct possibility in 1917.

It is possible to argue that mines subsequently failed to play as significant a role as they had during the First World War. In the Second World War, for example, mines were important in that they caused considerable loss, tied down vast resources to the task of clearing them and generally had a very important disruptive effect, but these accomplishments do not match the achievements of the mine in the earlier global conflict. German minefields in the First World War negated

44

British naval power in the southern North Sea and to a large extent contributed to the tying down of the British fleet for the duration of the war. In the Channel allied minefields made a vital contribution to the curbing of the U-boat menace. By comparison with these well-known examples of the role of mines in the First World War it is all too easy to forget that in 1915 a single line of mines laid in one very narrow stretch of water probably proved the most destructive and significant ever sown and possibly - though this is dubious - affected the outcome of the war itself. The Anglo-French naval attempt to force the passage of the Dardanelles on 18 March 1915 was a disastrous failure, the two navies between them losing four pre-dreadnought battleships to a combination of Turkish gunfire and mines. The attacking naval forces failed to break through the Dardanelles to Constantinople because the Turkish guns and mines complemented one another. The mines prevented allied warships from closing the range and smothering shore batteries with fire while the guns prevented the mines being swept, a foolproof defensive arrangement for which there was no answer other than the clearing of Turkish shore positions from landward. The March failure led directly to the amphibious operation to secure Gallipoli, and the campaign ended indecisively, with incalculable results for the conduct of the war in eastern Europe.

But if the mine indeed failed to play so significant a strategic role after 1918 as it did during the First World War, then it was not for want of effort and ingenuity on the part of the navies of the world. Mines in the Second World War were far more diverse than they had been during the 1914-1918 conflict, and they were used in greater numbers and in many distant waters that had been unvisited by hostilities in the previous war. The Germans, for example, laid minefields as far afield as the Cape and Australia. The development of the South African navy in the course of the war was overwhelmingly geared to harbour defence and minesweeping, and this development pointed to the very simple fact that for a relatively small outlay of human, capital and material resources a nation using mines offensively could tie down disproportionately large enemy forces for the continuous task of trying to keep the sealanes clear. When war broke out the Royal Navy deployed 75 minesweepers, but within a year this number had risen to almost 700 while by 1945 the British deployed 274 fleet minesweepers and 443 smaller minesweepers. A considerable number of the 350 operational trawlers in the Navy were fitted for minesweeping, and various other auxiliaries were also in service. Perhaps as many as 1,500 vessels flying the White Ensign were involved in minesweeping at the end of the war, and in the duration of the conflict the British accounted for some 14,300 German mines. The Germans equally had their resources increasingly stretched by allied mining. In all the British laid over 260,000 mines in the course of the war, 185,000 of them in protective positions in allied-controlled waters. In the end the remainder, when considered alongside strategic and tactical airstrikes against German harbours and shipping, overwhelmed the assorted collection of seventy flotillas that the Germans at various times organised in an unavailing attempt to keep the coastal trade of occupied Europe moving. Similarly, at the end of the war American mining of the Sea of Japan in the course of Operation Starvation all but severed sea communications between Japan and the Asian mainland, but by that time the Japanese fighting and merchant fleets had been virtually destroyed by American naval aircraft and submarines.

Aircraft and submarines were the main means of laying mines offensively during the Second World War, but the problems of laying mines by aircraft were never more forcefully displayed than in November 1939 when a German 'secret weapon' - a magnetic mine - was dropped on a mudflat off Shoeburyness without the self-destruct mechanism being switched on. A British naval specialist walked to the mine at low tide and dismantled it, thereby revealing to the British all the secret German developments of a mine the British themselves had invented in 1918. The magnetic mine operated when the magnetism of a target cut across the lines of force of a magnet inside the mine itself - the same principle as used in the indicator loop detectors. Later, acoustic mines and pressure mines were developed, and subsequent refinements incorporated various combinations, such as acoustic-magnetic initiation. Influence mines proved very difficult to counter because of their sophistication. Acoustic mines were operated by the sound of propellers and engines activating a vibrator in the mine, the pressure mine by differential water pressure caused by a ship passing over the weapon. The countering of the magnetic and acoustic mines was simple in principle but slow and always fraught with danger in practice. Magnetic mines were countered by demagnetising individual ships and using magnetic sweeps to set off the mines. In restricted shallow waters low-flying aircraft with electrically-charged coils were used to detonate mines. Acoustic mines could be dealt with by sound-producing equipment, electromagnetic oscillators or explosive sweeps. The latter proved the most successful manner of dealing with pressure mines, but no completely effective allied answer to pressure mines was developed before the end of hostilities.

In the course of the War the British lost at least 534 ships of about 1,406,000 tons to mines, nearly all of the losses being suffered in home waters and more than 50 per cent (279 ships/52.25 per cent of 772,431 tons/54.94 per cent) being incurred in the first sixteen months of war. Allied mines were the greatest single cause of German merchant losses, and, indeed, of German surface warship losses. Of the 1,821 ships of 3,230,129 tons lost by the German merchant fleet, 604 ships (33.17 per cent) of 660,533 tons (20.49 per cent) were lost to mines. Except in the disastrous year of 1944 when German defeats on land resulted in the loss of the French Atlantic and Mediterranean coasts and much of the Baltic and the complete loss of the Black Sea and lower Danube, losses to mines in every year exceeded losses to any other cause. The European axis powers also lost 973 warships of 924,058 tons, and of these totals mines accounted for 251 warships (25.80 per cent) of 160,730 tons (17.39 per cent).

This amount of destruction, though not in the end strategically significant, was a very fair return for what was a relatively small effort on the part of various navies, but it was small in comparison to the destruction wrought by submarines in the course of two World Wars. The submarine and torpedo in both conflicts posed the most serious and sustained of the underwater challenges to the freedom of movement of merchantmen and fighting ships alike, but with one exception submarines in the end failed to register strategic success.

The submarine and torpedo were both developed in the last four decades of the nineteenth century, the latter pre-dating the submarine to the extent that its initial means of delivery was provided by small purpose-built boats and then ships deliberately conceived to counter the threat of such craft (the destroyer). The torpedo was invented in the year of Lissa by the Austrians, another instance of a minor naval power leading the way in development designed to secure some measure of naval power at low cost. The torpedo's great asset lay in that it was an active weapon, unlike the mine, since it could be aimed deliberately at an enemy. Naturally, prototypes were very unreliable, slow and weak in explosive charge, but only twelve years separated its invention from the torpedo's first victim, the *Intikbah*, a Turkish guardship at Batum. Two Russian ships, the *Tchesma* and *Sulina*, closed to 80 yards to sink the 2,000-ton warship during the night of 26/27 January 1878.

The Russians had to close to such suicidal ranges because of the limitations of their weapons, but in the course of time the 'locomotive torpedo' gradually and significantly improved its performance. Contra-rotating propellers served to steady the torpedo on course, but not until the invention of the gyroscope in the mid-1890s was there any guarantee of reasonable accuracy. But even before the *Intikbah* was sunk one refinement had been developed that was to have immense repercussions. This was the balanced horizontal rudder that for the first time provided an answer, though only a partial one, to the problem of accurate and steady depth-keeping. The significance of this technological breakthrough was that it provided one of the critical inventions that made the submarine a practical proposition. What held back the development of the submarine until the late nineteenth century was not a lack of ingenuity and effort - amazingly, fourteen patents had been registered in England alone before 1727 - but a lack of suitable building material, power plant, controls and a weapon. The invention of the balanced rudder in 1877 was a solution to one of these difficulties, all of which were resolved by 1897.

It is perhaps surprising to realise just how far submarine development had progressed even before the submarine claimed its first victim in war as long ago as 1864. As early as the War of American Independence (1776-1783) a submarine attack had been carried out by an American vessel against a British warship, the *Eagle,* in New York. The means of attack was a powder keg to be screwed on to the bottom of the ship and a time fuse to set off the charge while the aptly-named *Turtle* withdrew. The attack was foiled by the *Eagle*'s copper sheath, and the charge had to be simply dropped and exploded without effect. In the War of 1812 the inventor of the *Turtle,* David Bushnell, tried again with a similar craft, but her attack on the *Ramillies* failed when the screw broke after having penetrated the copper bottom. Though another American, Robert Fulton, who worked at various times for both the French and British during the French Revolutionary and Napoleonic wars, managed to destroy practice targets in trials for both governments, nothing came of his experiments and it was not until 17 February 1864 when the Union sloop *Housatonic* was sunk in Charleston harbour by the Confederate *H. L. Hunley* that the first surface ship was claimed by a submarine. The *Housatonic* did have the posthumous satisfaction of taking her assailant with her, however, since the *Hunley* failed to survive her own success.

The *Hunley* episode was the climax of successive endeavours to counter Union supremacy at sea, the Confederate development of the submarine like the American and French beforehand being an attempt by the weaker side to devise an unorthodox response to enemy superiority. Such attempts were to prove unsuccessful, partly because of the inescapable fact that there is no effective substitute for balanced conventional power at sea, but mainly because of the limitations of technology at that time. But by 1864 certain basic ideas about submarines had been established. Fulton had devised his *Nautilus* in metal (copper plates on an iron frame) and had adapted a mid-eighteenth-century experiment that had submerged a wood and leather craft by admitting water into goatskin bags and raised it to the surface by expelling it by mechanical pressure. Fulton incorporated ballast tanks, compressed air and, moreover, a conning tower complete with glass porthole by which to navigate. A very primitive horizontal rudder was devised for steering and depth-keeping - a forerunner of the 1877 version - but what really confounded Fulton's inventiveness was the lack of a suitable weapon and means of propulsion. All the early submarines were hand-cranked and this gave them very little power of movement. Until some means of powered propulsion evolved the submarine's effectiveness was very slight because it could not hope to overhaul a ship.

Fulton's solution to this problem was steam power, and this indeed was tried in many nineteenth century developments in various countries. The attempts, however, always encountered the insoluble problem that if a steam boiler continued in use underwater it exhausted the air supply in no time at all, but if the fires were damped down before submerging the pressure remaining in the boilers was sufficient for only a very limited range. Compressed air engines, tried in the 1864 French *Le Plongeur,* similarly encountered the latter problem while the British use of electric motors in the 1866 *Nautilus* likewise suffered from the rapid exhaustion of the power source.

But the British had been working in the right direction, and in the next two decades the breakthrough came with the construction of two separate forms of propulsion, one when on the surface and one for when the submarine was submerged. Electric power was the only suitable means of underwater propulsion, and this came to be recognised by most navies though as late as 1900 the French were still conducting tests with steam power. The critical breakthrough came when two Americans, Simon Lake and John Holland, working separately, introduced petrol engines as the power pack for the submarine when on the surface. Paradoxically, in view of their persistence with steam, it was the French who took this development one step further and came up with a 'safe' method of surface propulsion in 1905 in the form of diesel engines on board the *Aigrette*.

It was Holland, however, who is generally credited with the development of the submarine since his craft, built in 1897 and accepted by the US Navy in 1900, contained all the ingredients (except two) of a proper underwater weapons system. The *Holland* incorporated dual-propulsion, horizontal rudder and ballast tanks to control diving, surfacing and underwater travel, compartmentalisation between engine, control and weapons room and, above all, suitable offensive armament. She carried a single bow torpedo tube with two reloads and two fixed-position guns. The British, nervously following developments and apprehensive because of the obvious threat such boats presented to their surface supremacy, bought a *Holland* and improved it by adding a periscope and conning tower. When the French introduced diesel engines as the surface power-pack, navies thereafter had the ingredients for successful submarine construction.

For more than half a century submarines showed no qualitative advance over the 8.5-knot 105-ton *Holland*. Submarines became far more sophisticated with the passing of the years, but until the harnessing of nuclear power as the means of propulsion in USS *Nautilus* in the mid-'fifties, the submarines of the world were recognisably the same as the nine-man *Holland* of 1897. Range had grown to the extent that the Pacific could be crossed in a single voyage. The number of torpedoes had increased more than ten-fold in forty years and there had been a period when even aircraft had been carried in submarines, some of which displaced over 6,000 tons. Speeds had risen less dramatically but towards the end of the Second World War the Germans had developed a new fuel, Ingolin, to secure exceptionally high underwater speeds from a gas-driven closed-circuit turbine. Even these developments, however, failed to alter the fact that the balance of naval technology had shifted decisively against the submarine in the course of the Second World War and that the most intensive guerre de course ever waged had been defeated by the combined efforts of the navies of the western allied nations.

Submarines, like so many other new weapons, encountered problems of employment from the start. No one had any real idea how best to use them. For the best part of three decades this situation remained unchanged until a German naval officer, Döenitz, began to set down a coherent strategic and tactical doctrine that he was to put into effect after 1939. The Japanese, similarly, evolved a coherent doctrine concerning submarine use in the inter-war period, but this was to be diametrically opposed to German concepts. The manner in which these two nations developed comprehensive strategic doctrines reflected their position of inferiority at sea vis-à-vis their potential enemies since both attempted to develop concepts of submarine warfare that compensated for their geographical and numerical weaknesses.

Japanese concepts envisaged the use of submarines in a purely military context. In this the Japanese never really advanced from the general concepts that were held by all navies before 1914. Where the Japanese added precision, however, was in the place that the submarine occupied within their general strategic concepts because their submarines were assigned specific tasks that had to be fulfilled if Japanese plans of expansion were ever to be realised. Because of this, and because the Japanese thus evolved concepts of submarine warfare that were very different from those of other nations, Japanese ideas will be examined in detail before we return to submarine development in the rest of the world.

In the inter-war period the Imperial Navy paid ever more attention to the likelihood of a war in the Pacific against the Americans. In 1941 the Navy settled for war in the belief that hostilities were inevitable and that war had best come sooner rather than later when American preparations were complete. Even then not a few Japanese commanders were aware of the very real prospect that Japan might well be dragged down to defeat by the sheer weight of the industrial resources that would be ranged against her, but by that stage there was nothing that they could do to prevent a drift into war. Even their more sanguine colleagues knew that a war with the Americans posed very grave dangers and, indeed, was likely to prove the most dangerous war Japan had ever fought, but they relied upon German success in Europe and the ability of their own capital ships and light forces to fight the Americans to exhaustion in the mid- and western Pacific.

It is always important to remember that the Japanese never envisaged their being able to defeat the US Navy. They aimed to maintain a force 50 per cent of the size of the American fleet and use their aircraft and submarines to wear down American strength in the western and central Pacific.

To plan to fight a war of attrition against the most industrialised society in the world and to believe that such a war could be prosecuted successfully despite a 2:1 inferiority to an enemy who could mount operations at times and places of his own choosing are notions that would make any western staff officer reach for his rum bottle in an effort to obliterate the suicidal implications of such a line of thinking. When it is realised that the Japanese planned to fight defensively, the initiative having been ceded, behind a defensive perimeter some 8,000 miles long, then Japanese strategic thinking in this period seems flawed, to say the least. But the concept begins to make sense within a mentality that stressed moral, surprise and qualitative factors as being supreme in war-making. Japanese martial fervour, the willingness of the soldier to die in the service of a divine emperor, was the basis of the moral superiority over their enemies that the Japanese believed would see them through against the odds. More specifically and practically the Japanese relied upon a qualitative superiority of their individual ships - the *Yamato*-class was deliberately bigger than any ship able to use the Panama Canal - and two other aspects of policy. Firstly, the Japanese relied on striking a paralysing blow in the opening attack. In Japanese swordsmanship there is a blow called the *iai*. It is a blow that is struck without any of the preliminary ritual and ceremony of combat and is a surprise blow delivered (by a right handed swordsman) in a single sweep as the sword leaves the sheath and cuts upwards from the opponent's right hip to left

51

shoulder. The iai-type blow that the Japanese were determined to strike was against the American Pacific Fleet at Pearl Harbor, leaving (it was believed) the Americans demoralised and bewildered and the owners of a broken-back fleet, just as the Chinese and Russians had been left after the Japanese had begun their wars of 1894 and 1904 (respectively) with surprise pre-emptive attacks. Secondly, to deal with any subsequent American thrust that might materialise across the Pacific the Japanese intended to use light, cheap craft, capable of quick and easy replacement, at the points of contact with the enemy to wear down the latter's strength. This phase envisaged Japanese light forces either defeating an enemy or inflicting disproportionately heavy losses on him to the extent that he would be left vulnerable to counter-attack by Japanese battle forces operating from the Japan-Marianas-Carolines-Marshalls complex. The forces regarded as expendable within this strategic concept were aircraft and submarines.

Japanese submarines in the course of 1940 had their operational areas extended as far east as Pearl Harbor itself and indeed some Japanese commanders expected their submarines to be more successful than their aircraft during the iai-style attack of 7 December 1941. For the enterprise the Japanese deployed 28 submarines off Hawaii with two more watching other American fleet anchorages. This amounted to half their total submarine force. On the day these submarines achieved nothing and the only success that all these submarines achieved in their first missions of the war was when one of their number torpedoed but failed to sink the aircraft carrier *Saratoga* in January off Oahu.

The use of submarines against enemy battle strength in an effort to equalise accounts before a fleet engagement lay at the heart of Japanese strategy. It had to be, because of Japanese numerical inferiority. The Japanese planned to use their submarines in a fleet reconnaissance role and as part of a fleet action, and their obsession with battle led them to neglect the use of submarines against lines of communication. No navy neglected the obvious point that submarines had a role to play in a reconnaissance role, and all were prepared to see their submarines engage opportunity targets, but the general balance of submarine doctrine in the rest of the world has shifted away from a fleet role.

Before the First World War all nations had thought of using submarines in a fleet role, but one man, Balfour, one-time prime minister of Britain, glimpsed the possibility of the submarine conducting a guerre de course against British trade. He saw this as the only sensible use of the submarine, and he tried to persuade Fisher, on two separate occasions First Sea Lord, of the correctness of this view. Fisher's conversion to Balfour's perception was belated. He grasped the implications of

Balfour's idea only in the weeks immediately before the start of the First World War. In this he was a matter of a few months in front of the German naval staff.

The German conversion to the cause of waging submarine warfare against trade was slow and very hesitant, and for good reason. When they went to war the Germans saw submarines as a complement to mines in their efforts to write down British naval strength before battle, and the urge to battle was the cornerstone of German naval doctrine (but only under certain conditions, as we have seen). When the British failed to impose close blockade, German submarines had to venture ever further afield in an effort to find prey. With the British employing distant blockade and moving their fleet only en masse and at high speed, submarines had little chance to scout effectively and inflict appreciable loss. But it was inevitable that at some stage a submarine would either accidentally sink a merchantman or capture and destroy one that was found to be carrying contraband as defined by the Declaration of London, 1909. (This Declaration the British signed but refused to ratify and ignored in the course of the war.) Only then did the realisation of the possibilities of a submarine guerre de course dawn on the German naval staff which then became converted to the prosecution of a *guerre à outrance* with their submarines against British trade.

But in the formulation of national strategy military deliberations could not have the final word. Unrestricted submarine warfare was a highly political issue since it was certain to involve moral issues and the question of German relations with neutrals whose ships were certain to be sunk in the course of such a campaign. The lengthening of the war into the foreseeable future and the German Army's increasing despair in 1915 and 1916 of being able to achieve victory lessened the importance of the moral argument for the Germans, particularly as the British blockade began to bite after 1915. But the matter of relations with neutrals was critical and complicated. On one side of a developing argument was a naval staff that argued that since a long war was certain to result in the progressive crippling of Germany, only an unrestricted submarine campaign offered Germany any hope of victory. The naval staff calculated that Britain relied for her imports on 6,750,000 tons of British shipping, 3,000,000 tons of neutral shipping and 1,000,000 tons of allied merchantmen. The staff came to estimate that the restricted campaigns of 1915 and late 1916 (after Jutland) had accounted for 400,000 tons of shipping a month and that submarines, if acting without restrictions, could sink a monthly average of 600,000 tons of merchantmen. The staff calculated that losses of this order would drive off the neutrals and see Britain forced out of the war in six months. In effect the staff rationalised a knee-jerk reaction to its own hopeless strategic situation and British blockade by elaborating a sea denial concept aimed at disrupting British command of the sea. The German civilian authorities, on the other hand, fought an increasingly desperate rearguard action in late 1916 against the Navy's demand. They argued, quite correctly, that the Navy's calculations were highly suspect, based as they were on dubious estimations of British losses during restricted campaigns (the staff did over-estimate by 30.76 per cent) and on the faulty assumption that Germany would be able to deploy an ever-growing strength continually at sea. The Chancellor, Bethmann-Hollweg, argued that the Navy's assumption that the British would not come up with some counter to the submarine threat was wrong, and he predicted that Britain would not weaken her resolve to retain command of the sea. Underlying all the civilian fears, however, was the prospect of provoking neutral, particularly American, intervention. This, the German civilian authorities knew, would doom Germany.

Unfortunately for Germany the civilians lost the argument, mainly because their views were defensive and negative and failed to offer any alternative to a course certain to end in Germany's exhaustion and defeat. The Navy's figures could not be disproved, and no one really knew what an unrestricted campaign might or might not achieve since such a campaign had never been fought. Fear of American power was easily brushed aside by the assertion that Britain would be beaten to her knees before American involvement had time to be effective. In the final weeks of argument the lure of the prospects of victory overrode a prudence that could only end in defeat - a defeat that was the inevitable result of pre-war German recklessness that had forced the world's greatest imperialist sea power to array herself with Germany's enemies.

It is hard not to feel sympathy with both sides of this argument, particularly when it is realised that in beginning unrestricted submarine warfare on 1 February 1917 the Germans pre-dated the first Russian Revolution of 1917 by a matter of weeks. The long hoped-for break in the ranks of Germany's enemies came just after the Germans had committed the one act that was all but certain to bring the USA into the war against her - thus for the Germans snatching defeat out of the jaws of victory in 1918. But the German failing was far deeper than that. The simple truth of the situation was that the Germans had managed to get themselves into a disastrous strategic position as a result of their own myopia and their failure to defeat France in 1914. Leaving aside the latter point, there was no denying the simple fact that the German authorities, and particularly the naval staff, never once thought through a coherent strategic doctrine either before or during the war. The obsession with the creation of a fleet for political reasons (and the assumption of a quick victory on land) obscured proper analysis of what would happen in the event of a war in which Britain chose not to stand aside but join Germany's foes: Britain's position as the world's greatest sea power gave her the choice of either appeasing or opposing Germany, and this the Germans forgot. There was no appreciation of what Germany should do in the event of Britain not imposing close blockade, even though such a blockade was increasingly unlikely, given the existence of mines and submarines. There was no examination of what even the most successful fleet action against the British would achieve for Germany. During the war the naval staff seized upon a dubious belief, belied by historical evidence, and imposed it upon authorities which proved more perceptive in their analysis of power and the deeper tide of human affairs. At every turn the German Navy showed a tactical and technical expertise that in many cases shamed the British, but this proficiency was never matched by political, strategic and moral astuteness. It is difficult to resist the notion that in this the Germans showed that navies are more than just a collection of ships, however good their characteristics. Ships and fleets can be built in a single generation; but navies worthy of the name cannot be created over-night. In the same way an enemy's command of the sea, when backed by geographical, numerical and psychological superiority, cannot be broken by a strategic concept that sets out to inflict cumulative damage that, by definition, needs time to take its toll.

By a very narrow margin the German unrestricted submarine campaign failed, but the failure was decisive in that it provoked the American intervention that alone held the Anglo-French armies in the field during the disastrous spring of 1918. After the collapse of Russia the only thing that stiffened British and French resolve was the knowledge that the Americans would arrive. The irony of this was that this failure occurred in spite of the fact that the U-boats sank on average more than 600,000 tons of merchantman a month for six months.

As Bethmann-Hollweg predicted, Britain was determined to retain command of the sea, and in April 1917 she was forced to adopt convoy in a last desperate attempt to stave off a defeat that then seemed inevitable and imminent. In February 1917 600 neutral merchantmen in Britain refused to sail and the number of sailings into Britain in the first quarter of 1917 fell by nearly 74 per cent from the total one year earlier. Sailings from Britain similarly showed a fall of nearly 72 per cent. In February the U-boats accounted for 234 ships of 532,856 tons, in March 281 ships of 599,854 tons and in April a staggering 373 ships of 869,103 tons while the merchantman:submarine loss exchange rate rose from 53:1 to 74:1 to 167:1 in those three months. But no other single set of events in the war at sea better illustrated the unchanging nature of strategy than the introduction of convoy. Convoy had been compulsory in the Age of Sail for British ships because it was recognised to be the best means of ensuring the safety of merchantmen on the high seas. It was a fact that was forgotten in the Age of Steam, but its reintroduction in 1917 saved the allies from defeat.

The basic strategic concept behind convoy was that the most reliable means of ensuring the safe arrival of merchantmen that would otherwise be vulnerable to attack by a well-armed raider was their concentration under the protection of warships. In this manner merchantmen would be escorted for the duration of their voyage, and a raider would have to deal with the escort if it wished to attack the merchantmen. The weakness of convoy was that it concentrated a large number of very valuable targets and if the escorts for some reason failed to defend their charges, a disaster of the first magnitude invariably ensued. The Dutch, for example, suffered appallingly in 1665 when the English overwhelmed their fighting escort and took or destroyed 180 merchantmen out of a convoy of 200. The British, similarly, had such disasters, amongst their worst being the loss in 1694 at French hands of 84 merchantmen from a convoy from Smyra. But even including these disasters men in the Age of Sail knew that a merchantman under escort was far safer than one sailing independently along a trade route dictated by prevailing winds. The figures proved it. Ships that deliberately sailed alone or straggled suffered far heavier losses than those that put on no pretence of bravery but nestled down under naval protection. Insurers knew this too since rates for ships sailing independently were much higher than those in convoy.

The coming of steam led the British to repeal their compulsory convoy regulations in the belief that mechanically-powered propulsion freed merchantmen from set courses. This remained one of the main arguments of those opposed to the reintroduction of convoy in 1917 while supporting arguments were provided by the belief that there were simply too many ships to be protected, ports would become too congested and valuable working days would be lost because of the need to concentrate shipping prior to sailings. It was also believed that merchantmen could not show the discipline needed to sail in convoy.

The British Admiralty persistently refused to incorporate convoy on ocean routes right up until April 1917 despite all the evidence of its effectiveness even in the limited instances where it was used beforehand. Troop movements were always in convoy, and not one transport was lost in the Channel between the outbreak of war and 1917. The Grand Fleet itself moved as a convoy, and in the whole of the war it lost just two light cruisers to submarine attack. These two instances were proof of the effectiveness of convoy, but there were even more dramatic instances of convoy's effectiveness. In response to crippling losses on the coal trade to France at the end of 1916 the British were forced to introduce convoy in February 1917. Losses that had been running at nearly 25 per cent were slashed almost to zero overnight. In all 37,927 sailings were completed under protection and only 53 colliers (0.14 per cent) were lost in 1917-1918. In July 1916 (i.e. before the start of convoy on the French trade routes) convoy had been introduced on the very vulnerable Anglo-Dutch routes, and two weeks after the start of the French coal convoys the first Anglo-Norwegian convoys were begun on a route that had seen 25 per cent losses as a regular occurrence. In all these cases convoy had been introduced in an effort to minimise unacceptably high losses, with success. There was an overwhelming body of evidence, even in the war, for the introduction of oceanic convoy, but this the Admiralty refused to accept.

Perhaps the best argument in favour of convoy was that it would immediately force the Germans to alter their methods of attack. It is perhaps surprising to realise that the vast majority of the merchantmen sunk in the war were not despatched by torpedoes but by gunfire and scuttling charges. Torpedoes were expensive and submarines carried few of them. As long as ships sailed independently submarines could stop and then sink them at very low cost with deliberate fire or by boarding. Convoy forced the submarine to use its limited supply of torpedoes to claim victims with no guarantee that each torpedo would claim a victim. Convoy thus reduced the offensive capability of U-boats and, moreover, embodied the offensive-defensive principle whereby the submarine had to expose itself to possible retribution if it sought prey. Submarines had to enter waters patrolled by the escorts, and there they were vulnerable. The earlier British practice of patrolling sea lanes did not achieve this. A submarine could simply submerge on sighting an enemy and evade him: there was no need to attack a warship that had a longer endurance and was protecting nothing. The submariner knew that sooner or later unescorted merchantmen would appear and could be picked off one by one. Convoy ended this advantage. It gave the submarine just one chance of sighting and forced it to run the gauntlet of the escorts if it was to claim victims. This basic concept went unquestioned in Nelson's time, but it was rejected in an era obsessed with material and technological development. The period before the First World War, even allowing for the influence of such writers as Corbett and Mahan, was one when naval thought languished. One acid commentator of this era has observed that naval theory consisted of a few catchwords and a lot of tradition.

This paralysing conservatism that fixed upon the very worst aspects of tradition at the expense of clear and rational thought brought Britain within measurable distance of defeat in 1917. There seemed no limit to the destructiveness of submarines other than their own weapons capacity and endurance. But the British Admiralty was forced to do so on the direct orders of the prime minister, Lloyd George. Subsequently the Admiralty claimed that it had already been converted to the cause of convoy before the famous meeting with Lloyd George in April, but there is no real doubting to whom the credit for the introduction of convoy should go - or whom the Admiralty would have blamed had convoy for some reason failed to stem British losses: Lloyd George.

But convoy did not fail, despite the continued efforts of the Admiralty. Rather than escorting ships into harbour at first the Admiralty insisted that convoys were dispersed in the western approaches and left to make their own ways to port. Many ships that had safely made their way across the Atlantic succumbed on the very last lap of their voyage, precisely because of the obstructiveness and lack of forethought on the part of the Admiralty. It was not until November that convoy directly into British ports was instituted, by which time oceanic convoy had been in effect in both directions across the Atlantic for some three months.

Convoy in fact proved remarkably effective in reducing allied losses and causing casualties amongst the hitherto almost invulnerable U-boats. Both were to be critically important in breaking the submarine menace but it was the former, the containing of losses to bearable proportions, that was more important. Before the introduction of the first oceanic convoy in May 1917 - on the Gibraltar-Britain route - merchantmen had a one in four chance of being sunk during an Atlantic crossing, but these odds rose considerably as the merchantman:submarine loss exchange rate shrank to 10:1 by the end of the year. In the course of the war 16,070 ships sailed in oceanic convoys with a loss of just 96 of their number (0.60 per cent) while 161 merchantmen (0.24 per cent) were lost from the 67,880 sailings that at various times made up British coastal convoys. Losses amongst ships that broke convoy or which continued to sail alone and after convoy dispersal continued to be high, but never high enough to give Germany hopes of victory. Indeed, Germany for much of the time was losing ground. Allied financial power enabled them to charter neutral shipping to tide them over the critical period of spring 1917 while in 1918 losses were more than offset by new construction. In the last year of the war allied shipyards produced 4,000,000 tons of new merchantmen, just over 1,250,000 tons more than U-boat sinkings. The convoy strategy was equally effective against mines. A convoy could be routed through waters which were known to be cleared: an antidote to mines which was re-learnt in the Second World War.

German submarine losses also rose, the Germans losing 178 of their 373 U-boats in the course of the war. But for only one brief period between August 1917 and January 1918 did their losses exceed their new construction (46 to 42). Much of this can be ascribed to the Germans' natural problem of having to adjust to new tactical requirements and suffering in the meantime. In the course of 1918 German losses were high but not intolerably so. What this fact pointed to was the unmistakable conclusion that in the First World War the submarine threat was contained rather than defeated and that strategic factors rather than tactical and technical aspects were the decisive features in the submarines' failure to achieve the results expected and demanded by the German naval staff. In part this failure came about, as the German civilian authorities had argued, from the inability of submarines to operate at full capacity all the time. Their deployment on patrols tended to be cyclical. Much of the initial devastating success registered in the first three months of the unrestricted campaign stemmed from the fact that the Germans had been able to prepare for a given moment with their full strength, but by May the Germans had the utmost difficulty in maintaining 29 submarines at sea. By August sufficient regrouping and preparation had been carried out for seventy submarines to be at sea, the highest monthly total of the war, but if the Germans were to have won this campaign then they needed this level of strength at sea at all times, not as a result of a supreme effort. The small number of submarines that the Germans had available at any one time during 1917 was not enough to make an unrestricted campaign work because a sufficiently high rate of continuous loss could not be inflicted on regrouped British resources. To this basic fact must be added certain other strategic failures and weaknesses. The German failure to concentrate all their submarines against trade in the Atlantic, the closing of the Dover Strait, the allied cutting of their own losses and their replacement capabilities were all contributing factors to the blunting of the U-boat challenge in 1917-1918.

But if strategic factors had largely determined the outcome of the campaign, the tactical situation was not decisively clear-cut either in favour of the escorts or the submarines. The submarines had failed to sink sufficient escorted merchantmen to earn their keep, but the escorts had similarly failed to inflict significant defeat on the opposition. Both sides had good cause to consider the future possibilities, but in the inter-war period the Royal Navy believed that it had the antidote to the submarine in the form of an effective detection device and a good reliable weapon. The means of detection was ASDIC, developed during the war and named after the organisation responsible for its invention, the Allied Submarine Detection Investigation Committee. ASDIC, now known as 'sonar', was an active electronic search device that emitted pulses of high frequency sound from a housing carried on the bottom of an escort. These pulses would bounce back to the escort when they encountered an underwater object, the range of the object being determined by the length of time that passed between transmission and reception. Some of the problems associated with sonar were that it could give echoes from various forms of marine life, its effectiveness could be drastically reduced by thermal layers in the sea and it could only operate below certain depths. This meant that an escort lost contact with a submarine as it ran in to deliver an attack with the weapon that was a proven submarine-killer, the depth-charge. The latter was a high-explosive charge designed to be fired by a hydrostat at a given depth, the weapon relying on shock effect through water rather than the immediate force of the explosion to break open the submarine.

Sonar represented a formidable advance over the hydrophones which had previously been the only means of detecting submerged U-boats. Hydrophones were passive and to be effective an escort had to either stop or move at extremely low speeds in order to hear the sound of a submarine's propellers. By using a number of escorts to listen and plot the direction of the source of sound an accurate fix could be secured, and the submarine could then be attacked. The *UC-7* gained the unenviable distinction of being the first submarine to be lost to the hydrophone/depth-charge combination in July 1916, just a little more than three months after depth-charges claimed their first victim when the Q-ship *Farnborough* lured *U-68* to destruction on 26 March.

Time was to show that the combination of sonar and depth-charges was a very formidable one, but not before certain of their limitations had been painfully revealed. Amongst its most serious weaknesses was sonar's very strength, its ability to detect a submerged object. It could not detect an object very near or on the surface, and this weakness was vitally important in the light of new concepts of conducting submarine operations that were being devised in Germany in the inter-war period by Döenitz.

Döenitz was behind the development of new tactical concepts of submarine warfare but, of course, he did not function in a political and strategic void. He was a member of a Navy that after 1919 was in desperate need of a role and a sensible reasoned strategy. It aspired to regain world status and power, but for most of the inter-war period it barely had the capacity to operate effectively against even Poland. Its combat performance had been impressive, yet its influence on the outcome of the war had been disastrous. At the end of the war the German Navy was confronted with the very real intellectual problem of trying to understand why the Imperial Navy, which had cost so much to build, had achieved so little and just how, why and in what ways a new Kriegsmarine at some future date would be different.

In this period of re-evaluation the father of the Imperial Navy, Tirpitz, played an extremely pernicious and malevolent role. To him the failure of 'his' navy was very simple: he had not been in command of it. He placed responsibility for failure on the alleged personal shortcomings of its commanders whose timidity and lack of foresight led them to miss opportunities. In short, Tirpitz alleged that 'his' fleet had been misused and that no one had wielded it as an offensive weapon as he had intended. Nothing was further from the truth, but Tirpitz conducted a masterly campaign of self-justification through misrepresentation and distortion to conceal his own personal failings and to obscure the basic fallacy that undermined the whole raison d'etre of the German Navy. The fallacy, of course was that the creation of a fleet for political reasons without regard to its geographical, numerical and psychological inferiority to its opponents left it in a helpless strategic situation for which the desire to do battle was but the minimum tactical response to a lost strategic cause. Throughout the war the Imperial Navy remained a glorified coastal defence force despite its size. Its use of submarines for an offensive guerre de course was merely the instinctive reflex to its own strategic futility.

Tirpitz's campaign of self-justification through the ridicule and character-assassination of others served to confuse the new German Navy still more. What Tirpitz argued, in effect, was that more effort down the course he claimed to have plotted would have brought results, and it was not until 1926 that the course that Tirpitz had plotted was seriously questioned. In that year a retired Vice-Admiral, Wegener, served notice on the Tirpitz line, though he never indulged in the head-on assault on Tirpitz that alone would have dispelled the malignant lingering influence of his former chief. Wegener fixed attention for future strategic debate where it really mattered by arguing that sea warfare revolved around the struggle to control lines of communication and the defence of trade. To hammer home his message he pointed out that the search for a tactical success over the British fleet was valueless in a lost strategic situation. The North Sea, given Britain's geographical position, had no strategic value: a German victory there would lead nowhere. What Wegener did was to point out that the German Navy in the First World War had no reasoned strategic aim, and he brought home with unmistakable clarity and force that the German search for a means of bringing the British fleet to battle under circumstances most favourable to the High Sea Fleet was irrelevant when set against the problem of trying to maintain German lines of communication with the outside world.

Had Wegener left the argument at that point he would have made a major contribution to German strategic thinking by dragging the Navy away from the mental paralysis caused by its creation for political reasons and its obsession with battle. He would have brought his former service face to face with the massively complicated problem of its strategic mission. Unfortunately for the German Navy Wegener was not content with diagnosis, and his prescription turned out to be as disastrously erroneous as the concepts of Tirpitz had been. In this Wegener was culpably guilty of forcing through a partial view as a comprehensive account, but in truth this was not entirely his own fault. The German Navy was only too willing to be convinced, and the compelling logic of his initial arguments and premises did much to force through an uncritical acceptance of his dubious conclusions. Moreover, there were others, some of whom agreed with Wegener and others who did not, who helped to further confuse issues that in any event became ever more distorted by the rise of National Socialism.

To counter the British fleet's positional, numerical and psychological advantages over the German Navy Wegener argued that Germany should have occupied Denmark and southern Norway, thereby either breaking or pushing back the British blockade and giving direct access into the Atlantic. This 'solution' begged the real issue: it failed to get to grips with the impossible strategic position of a German fleet in a war with Britain because a German fleet off southern Norway would be in scarcely a better strategic position to protect trade than it would be operating from German ports. But the dangerous and disastrous implications inherent in Wegener's line of thought can be seen. In forcing attention to the strategic purposes of sea power (the maintenance of lines of communication), by pointing to just one aspect of a strategic situation (geographical position) to overcome wider strategic disadvantages and by shifting attention away from the tactical aspects of battle, Wegener opened up a perilous line of reasoning that was all the more insidious for its being argued so well to an illogical conclusion. Wegener argued that sea warfare was about lines of communication whereas it was concerned with command of the sea which is something more than lines of communication. He failed to see that sea warfare was about control of an enemy's movements as a means of breaking his lines of communication, and Wegener failed to appreciate the extent to which control of movement could depend on the outcome of battle. By pointing to a geographical shift of position to counter strategic inferiority he opened up a line of thought that had to lead, as it did, to the notion that command of the sea was something that was divisible and could be localised.

By being so accurate in so much of his analysis of what had gone wrong Wegener misled people into believing that he was correct in his recipe.

Worse was to follow because other historians and factors were at work in shaping the development of the new Navy. Wegener was not the only person who looked at the record and found the Tirpitz account wanting. Most important of Wegener's fellow thinkers was Assmann whose consideration of the triple weaknesses of the Imperial Navy - strategic position, numbers and lack of strategic purpose - tended to become obscured by his pre-occupation with blockade. Wegener, all through his writings, tended to confuse command of the sea with control of enemy forces and even with the struggle to secure command. He wrote as if the struggle for and exercise of command of the sea were one and the same thing, but Assmann drifted into an even more serious failing by going one stage further when he confused the very purpose of blockade. He does not seem to have realised that the switch from close to distant blockade was one of technique and means and that it was dictated by such mundane matters as mines and submarines. Assmann saw the switch as a change of role and function in British war-making from military to economic objectives. The ability to wage economic warfare as a result of controlling enemy fleet movements was not appreciated by Assmann who came to see naval warfare solely in terms of economic warfare in which it was not important for a land power to secure command of the sea for itself. By extension of the argument economic warfare was possible even without challenging an enemy's formal command of the sea - it was basically irrelevant - and in this context battle was to be avoided, not sought. In their very different ways, and it is hard to appreciate the extent to which Wegener and Assmann disagreed, the confused writings of these two men pushed the German Navy very slowly into accepting the absurd notion that command of the sea was simply and wholly identifiable with control of maritime communications, that war at sea was an economic contest shorn of military aspects, that avoidance of engagements was desirable since battle conflicted with the use of forces against economic objectives and that sea denial in terms of area and/or time was as effective as command itself.

When these points are tied in with the ideas of Hitler and the drift of events between 1933 and 1939 one can see that the German Navy, notwithstanding its confidence to win a war, was in as dangerous an intellectual position as it had been before 1914 because it lacked a rational strategic aim. Its strategic thinking centred around the belief that it could wage 'tonnage war' with an inferior (almost non-existent) force from a position of geographical disadvantage. The naval staff calculation was that if German raiders, mostly submarines, could sink

750,000 tons of British shipping a month for one year Britain would fall. It was the same line of reasoning as 1916-1917 but with a veneer of intellectual respectability that in fact reflected the shallowness of the Navy's strategic analysis. In effect Wegener and Assmann brought German naval thought back in a full circle. Hitler, of course, only aggravated the problem because his ideas, largely drawn from notions of geo-politics based on such sources as MacKindler, Kjellén and Haushofer, were centred on the notion that the struggle of the race to survive was territorial - of earth and blood - and not concerned with trade and the projection of power to overseas areas. Hitler might want a return of Germany's colonies, and a few more into the bargain, but in Nazi ideology the Aryan race earned its right to survive in the life and death struggle for central and eastern Europe with the Slavic *untermenschen*. To Hitler, therefore, the crime and folly of Imperial Germany had been its attempt to expand its industrial, trading and naval base at the expense of pursuing Germany's historic destiny in the east, and in doing so provoking Britain's enmity. The latter was something that Hitler was determined to avoid, and his obsession with this, when set alongside his overwhelming concern with territory and armies, inevitably resulted in the Kriegsmarine's relegation to a very low position on his list of priorities. Moreover, Hitler's own views on the nature of war itself served to reinforce the trends set by Wegener and Assmann. Hitler saw war not so much in terms of a military conflict but as an ideological struggle of global proportions in which economic factors but particularly political ingredients were decisive. War, to Hitler, was a total struggle for racial survival in which political and economic resources were all-important, the military aspects of conflict being the manifestation and reflection of will and power. Thus just as the effectiveness of the British blockade in the First World War had been crucial in shaping Assmann's analysis of strategy, so Hitler's view of the importance of economic power in the waging of war coincided with and reinforced the notion that the economic aspects of naval warfare was the be-all of conflict at sea. Given this situation, the role of heavy surface ships was obvious. Useful though they may be in the conduct of commerce war, their prime importance lay in being images of the power of the new Germany and the means of enhancing Germany's diplomatic position, just as the High Sea Fleet had been before 1914. Such a view precluded their being exposed to danger, their continued existence being more important than losses they might inflict.

Erroneous strategic concepts on its own part and unbalanced and unimaginative political leadership on the part of Hitler when it came to naval policy thus beset the Kriegsmarine throughout the Nazi era, but the real and significant damage they did to the German Navy was in the pre-war period. The Navy planned, in accordance with Hitler's instructions, for war for 1944, and it was given priority behind the Army and the Luftwaffe. It planned to build a balanced fleet by 1944 with the aim of waging all-out economic warfare, but the reckless drift of German policy in 1938-1939 brought about war when Germany had but 57 of the 300 U-boats the naval staff estimated were needed to bring Britain to her knees.

When one looks at a map of German conquests and a graph of allied shipping losses in the Second World War, and then at the comparative tables of area, population and production of Germany and her enemies, one is always struck not by the fact that Germany lost but that she came so close to winning. Of course Germany, in complete contrast to Britain, wins every battle except the last one, and herein lay the clue to the nature of the war at sea in the European context between 1939 and 1945. In both 1940 and 1941 the Germans sank about 4,150,000 tons of merchant shipping and almost doubled this achievement in 1942 when some 1,664 allied merchantmen of 7,790,697 tons were sunk. Of the 1942 totals 1,006 ships (60.46 per cent) were sunk in the North Atlantic and 1,160 (69.88 per cent) were sunk by submarines. In March 1943 the allies lost 627,377 tons of merchant shipping, the third highest monthly toll of the war, despite the fact that convoys were then being escorted in unparalleled strength. Indeed, the German success in March 1943 threatened the whole notion of convoy itself, and for the allies this was the crisis of the war at sea. Yet here was the nub of German weakness, even at the moment of great success, because April-May 1943 was the period when Germany had to pay the price for her mistakes as the tide of battle in the Atlantic turned decisively against her. If economic warfare was ever to have had a chance of success, the losses of 1942 needed to be registered in both 1940 and 1941, not 1942 by which time allied resources had been mobilised to the extent that such losses could be absorbed. A war of attrition could not work because it took too long to become effective and had to be waged single-handed by one arm of the Wehrmacht. Over-extension on other fronts led it to cut back a balanced construction programme that alone may have led to the dispersal of enemy effort that would have produced conditions of victory. It took until January 1942 for the Germans to raise the number of U-boats in service to 249 - they lost 58 in 1940 and 1941 - and it can be seen in retrospect that the Kriegsmarine was always two years behind its operational needs, and this time it could not recover. The total of 249 U-boats in service in January 1942 still allowed only 91 to be operational. By the time U-boat construction raised German strength to the levels deemed necessary to win the campaign the moment for doing so had passed.

That the U-boats were so successful for so long and came within measurable distance of success was largely the result of British weakness (and in 1942 the USA as well) and the effectiveness of U-boat tactical doctrine. There is the unconscious irony of history repeating itself in that the German Navy began two wars with confidence and a far better tactical doctrine than strategy. There is no denying that Döenitz had developed a concept of submarine warfare that proved remarkably effective. He did so by pinpointing the critical U-boat failing in the First World War, their lack of overall organisation. U-boats had operated individually, and only in the latter stages of the conflict had the Germans organised their submarines to search specific areas to locate enemy convoys. Döenitz took this process one step further by realising that it was inefficient for submarines to search for their own prey by areas. He organised U-boats into an extended line of search, submarines being stationed to provide overlapping arcs of vision, across the anticipated convoy route. At night this line cruised slowly away from a possible convoy, turning at dawn to resume a course to obtain contact. Upon contact a submarine made a sighting report and took up a position to continue to shadow and report the convoy, normally by diving deep and resurfacing astern of the convoy. Other submarines were directed against the convoy by submarine headquarters ashore, and attacks began when the attackers were concentrated in force to overwhelm the escorts. By attacking in 'wolf-packs' the submarines offered one another mutual protection, their very numbers all but ensuring that no escort had time to hunt down individual contacts to destruction because of the demands on her services to forestall other attacks. Normally submarine attacks were made on the surface, usually from astern which was the weak point of a convoy's defence, but this depended on such factors as sea conditions and moon. Surface attacks at night were reasonably safe because the low silhouette of a submarine made it very difficult to detect against the black background of the sea. Surface ships, on the other hand, stood out clearly against the horizon.

For the best part of three and a half years such tactics enjoyed great success, though even before April/May 1943 there were several pointers to the fact that their effectiveness could be countered under certain circumstances that were all too infrequently present on the allied side before 1943. These circumstances, however, prevailed in the last two years of war with the result that the German attempt to wage economic warfare was broken, in spite of the fact that in the course of hostilities the allies lost 5,150 merchantmen of 21,570,720 tons in all theatres from all causes. Submarines accounted for 2,828 ships (54.91 per cent) of

14,687,231 tons (68.09 per cent) with a total of 2,232 ships (43.34 per cent) of 11,899,732 tons (55.17 per cent) going to their last resting place in the Atlantic. Amidst such carnage and untold human misery there is an irony. Half a world away a submarine campaign that had not been pre-planned, which was infinitely less destructive in absolute terms and which was waged with far less strength than that deployed by Germany achieved strategically decisive results.

That campaign, of course, was the American submarine campaign against Japanese merchant shipping in the western Pacific. Its success was overshadowed by the great carrier battles of the Pacific campaign and the fact that the end of the war came in such an awesome manner with the destruction of Hiroshima and Nagasaki by nuclear weapons. But the fact of the matter was that even before Japan became the first victim of nuclear attack, she had been beaten to her knees and her naval power had been utterly annihilated by a combination of American naval aviation, surface ships and submarines.

It was an annihilation of Japanese naval power that encompassed the Imperial Navy, the merchant fleet, the ports and the industrial base that supported fighting and mercantile fleets alike. The destruction of the cutting edge of Japanese naval power at Midway, the Philippine Sea and Leyte Gulf is so well known as to need no further comment, but the scores of nameless encounters, fought with savage fury at night amid the islands of the south west Pacific, that wrote down Japanese light forces and the massacre of Japanese merchant shipping are less well known.

In the course of the Pacific war the Japanese lost 84.74 per cent of their merchant navy. Japan began the war with 6,051,660 tons of merchant shipping. A little known aspect of the Japanese decision to go to war was that in doing so Japan lost the services of 4,000,000 tons of merchant shipping of other nations that until that time carried cargoes without which Japan could not hope to survive. Japan salvaged and captured 822,963 tons of allied shipping. Thus the exchange rate for the five American battleships sunk at Pearl Harbor was about 3,200,000 tons of merchantmen, a ruinous rate of exchange for a nation which, like Britain, was totally dependent on the sea for her trade and capacity to wage war. Worse was to follow because while 3,293,314 tons of new merchant shipping was built by Japan in the course of the war, 8,618,234 tons were lost to all causes. Of this total submarines accounted for 1,153 ships (51.36 per cent) of 4,889,000 tons (56.73 per cent) of all Japanese losses.

American submarines were necessarily slow to get into their stride, but from the first day of the war they began to wage unrestricted war against Japanese commerce for the very simple reason that in the aftermath of the Pearl Harbor attack they were the only means of conducting offensive operations available to the Americans. Problems with torpedoes and the vast distances involved in Pacific operations hampered American efforts to start with, but American submarines began to exact an important toll of Japanese shipping. Japan's problems in this respect were compounded by the very poor planning of the use of her shipping resources, by a mistaken tactical doctrine that stressed patrolling as opposed to convoy and by the poor provision of escorts when convoy was at last introduced. The Japanese showed a poor appreciation of the importance of their merchant shipping and made fundamental, and irreversible, errors in their calculations concerning their tanker and oil capacities. They also badly miscalculated their building capacity and their possible losses since they believed that they could more than replace any loss they were likely to suffer. In fact Japanese captures, salvage and building proved sufficient to tide the Japanese over the first year of the war, but thereafter Japanese merchant losses escalated beyond replacement capacity as the Americans began to break into the defensive perimeter formed by the Japanese in the central and south-west Pacific. When this happened the Japanese had to send their merchantmen into waters controlled increasingly by American air power, with disastrous results. But even though aircraft were instrumental in breaking Japanese mercantile power during this phase of operations and at the very end of the war, submarines remained the means of continuous attrition which broke the back of the Japanese merchant fleet.

But the Pacific campaign was a poor reflection of the general balance between submarine and escort, between defence and attack. In simple terms the American success was achieved against an enemy who laboured under too many handicaps, technical, numerical and of his own tactical making, for any general conclusion to be drawn about the state of the art. In fact, the Americans, who lost just 52 submarines in the course of this campaign, achieved a result that could never have been registered in the Atlantic. The Battle of the Atlantic indeed showed that the technical balance had decisively shifted against the submarine. Admittedly, at the very end of the war new German submarines had been developed that threatened the supremacy that escorts had enjoyed since 1943, but in general terms the experience of this battle was that anti-submarine warfare had evolved to the point where submarines could no longer function effectively. The last two years of war showed that submarines laboured under insurmountable handicaps and that any attempt to increase their chances of survival could only be achieved at the price of an intolerable reduction of offensive power. That this was the case, that the most serious of the underwater challenges to the supremacy of the surface ship was broken, was in large part the result of the development of the third dimension of naval warfare that in its own right was to end the primacy of the surface warship - naval aviation.

CHAPTER IV

OUT OF SIGHT AND OVER THE SEA: AIRCRAFT

The curse of history is the manner in which popular demand necessitates identification of either 'turning-points' or the 'cause(s)' of the unfolding of events. History, invariably, is an intricate mosaic, and the search for the 'simple solution' as explanation of complicated human problems inevitably produces an answer that is neat, plausible and wrong. What is often identified as a 'turning-point' is, more often than not, the point where various trends and developments, some time in the making, can be said for the first time to be seen to be taking a hand in the shaping of events.

In no case is this more true than with regard to the outcome of the Battle of the Atlantic in the Second World War. The change of fortune in this battle can be, and often is, identified as having taken place in May 1943 when no fewer than 41 U-boats failed to return to base. Undoubtedly that month marked a dramatic point in the battle if only because German losses then were greater than their losses for the whole of both 1940 and 1941 and almost half their total 1942 losses. But the relevant facts make it clear that while the German losses in May 1943 were exceptionally severe, they were really part of a general if less spectacular trend that continued until the end of the war. U-boat losses for the whole of 1943 totalled 237 and rose to 242 in 1944. In 1945 the Germans lost a further 151 submarines up to and including 7 May while allied merchant losses, in contrast, were reduced to very low levels. In August 1943 only two allied merchantmen were lost in the North Atlantic, and between June 1943 and May 1944, only (sic) 442,684 tons of merchant shipping were lost in this theatre. In the last thirteen months of the war German submarines sank a total of 121 ships of 640,325 tons, a total slightly higher than their sinkings in March 1943 alone.

What these figures show is that the May 1943 events were part of a trend that in the last two years of war saw the comprehensive mastery of submarines by escorts in a manner never achieved in 1917-1918. German losses were too heavy and consistent and their rate of success was too small compared to their strength and losses for the U-boat losses to be explained in local, personal or tactical terms. In July 1944, for example, with 434 U-boats in commission of which 181 were operational, the Germans sank twelve merchantmen of 63,351 tons for the loss of 23 of their own number. There has to be a more general explanation for the process by which the submarine was transformed from being the instrument that in 1943 came close to breaking the convoy system and shattering allied command of the sea to its being no more than a minor irritant by 1945. While many factors were at work in bringing about this state of affairs, possibly the most important was the increasing number and effectiveness of allied aircraft in the battle.

At the end of the war the Germans surrendered 156 U-boats and scuttled another 221 to add to the 785 already destroyed in the course of the war. Of the latter total, 246 (31.34 per cent) were sunk by allied warships and another 21 (2.68 per cent) by submarines. Soviet action, accidents, mines and marine and unknown causes accounted for a further 118 (15.03 per cent). But 290 fell to shore- and ship-based aircraft while another 62 (7.90 per cent) were destroyed in strategic bombing raids. The balance of 48 submarines was shared between ships and aircraft. From these figures, therefore, it can be seen that excluding the destruction wrought by strategic bombing, aircraft accounted for 36.94 per cent of total U-boat losses and shared another 6.11 per cent with warships while aircraft-laid mines added another 16 U-boats, 219 German warships (147,625 tons) and 564 merchantmen (607,476 tons) to the tally. Of the fifteen largest German surface warships to see service nine were either sunk or damaged beyond repair by aircraft with one more, the *Bismarck,* shared with warships. On the other hand only two, the *Graf Spee* and *Sharnhorst,* succumbed as a result of surface action.

One further statistic is of interest. In 1942 and 1943 aircraft sank more U-boats than did the surface escorts. In 1943 aircraft accounted for 140 U-boats and shared another 13 with warships. This was a total only two less than U-boat losses from all causes between 1939 and 1942. The success of aircraft in 1943 completely overshadowed the warships' victories which amounted to 59, but in the last sixteen months of the war the balance of success narrowly favoured the warships. These statistics clearly show the extent of the aircraft's impact on the Battle of the Atlantic. The figures are also an important corrective to the inclination to see the story of naval aviation during the war in solely Pacific terms. Events in the Pacific tend to overshadow the success of aircraft in the naval battles in the European theatre of operations and the Atlantic. There is no denying that the impact of air power in the Pacific was more immediate and spectacular, but any examination of the role of naval aviation in the course of the Second World War must balance the part played by aircraft in fleet operations against the part they played in the no less important task of defending trade. It should also be remembered, moreover, that the latter was the field of activity where aircraft first 'won their spurs' in the First World War to the extent that but five merchantmen were lost from convoys that enjoyed air support. Moreover, in the critical period July-September 1917 when the issue was in the balance, aircraft accounted for five U-boats, almost one-third of the total German losses in that period. These achievements came at a time when both the range and striking power of aircraft were extremely limited.

It was this gradually increasing offensive capacity that lay at the heart of the arguments that raged in naval circles over the role of naval aviation in the period before 1941. What was evident by 1945 was not so clear before 1941 as naval men everywhere tried to balance the proven power of surface warships against the unknown qualities of aircraft, the essential problem being to decide not what an aircraft was capable of doing but what it was capable of doing in combat conditions and how this would affect strategic and tactical doctrine. Some admirals such as Fisher and Scott, ironically the big-gun men of the pre-1914 era, firmly believed that navies in future would, literally, take to the air. They believed that aircraft would make surface warships obsolete, but this was altogether too much for the overwhelming majority of naval officers. Most at this time felt that aircraft would have a very important role to play at sea but very few believed that aircraft would supersede the gun. In all countries the whole question of naval aviation was tied in with the wider issue of independent air forces and the idea of strategic bombing. These issues were made ever more complicated as every year brought improvements in the range, speed and weapons load of all types of aircraft.

This pace of advance was naturally greatest during the initial development of the aircraft after the first controlled flight by a heavier-than-air machine in December 1903 by Orville Wright in the USA. The distance flown on that occasion was a mere 820-ft, or less than the length of the future *Hood*, but by 1905 this had been pushed up to 24 miles and in 1908 a Frenchman, Louis Blériot, made the first flight across the Channel. The first night flight took place in 1910, the same year as the first flight across the North Sea, from Scotland to Norway, was made by a Norwegian, Tryggve Gran. The implications of this flight of more than four hours across nearly 300 miles of sea were obviously significant for navies. The first instance of the military use of aircraft came in 1912 when the Italians bombed Turkish troops with grenades, and, of prime significance for navies, on 28 July 1914, at the time that Europe slithered into war, a Short seaplane of the Royal Naval Air Service launched a 14-in 800-lb torpedo from the air, though the aircraft had to be specially lightened in order to do so.

Thus in its first ten years of life the aircraft showed amazing improvements in its speed, range and lift capabilities, but inevitably it remained a puny, unsophisticated and temperamental machine. One crusty British admiral was not being reactionary and unrealistic when he rejected the offer of aircraft for anti-submarine work on the grounds that he lacked spare ships to search for ditched aircrew.

In the course of the First World War heavier- and lighter-than-air machines complemented one another's efforts though they were rivals in the race to control the future of naval aviation. Both types had their limitations, and right until the end of the war lighter-than-air machines retained certain very marked advantages over their companions. Rigid and non-rigid airships possessed greater ranges and weapons loads than aircraft and they carried radios which made them far superior for scouting purposes to many types of heavier-than-air machines.

In airship technology Germany led the world. The German Navy used its airships for scouting, but for most of the war their results were unimpressive. They could always report the absence of ships from a given area, but at none of the capital ship engagements in the North Sea did airship reconnaissance play any part in operations. (On only one occasion, in August 1916 during the German sortie against Sunderland, did airship reconnaissance have any significant result, and then only through error. On that occasion false sighting reports resulted in a German change of plan that actually saved the High Sea Fleet from unknowingly being trapped by the Grand Fleet.) To counter German airships the British settled on developing heavier-than-air machines, its own airship programme being first scrapped and then revived at very low level. This decision was far-sighted and by the end of the war had begun to pay dividends, but it did not solve immediate technical problems concerning their operations that indeed were only satisfactorily resolved after the war.

These problems arose not because of any specialisation between types of heavier-than-air machines - for much of the war the distinction between fighters, scouts and bombers was marginal - but because of the limitations of aircraft and seaplanes alike. Aircraft, operating from shore bases, were too few in number and too limited in range and offensive power to perform anything more than a limited coastal patrol role. Patrolling aircraft escorted the Grand Fleet to sea for the first time on 27 August 1914, but their range was so limited that in reality all they could provide was partially effective air cover when there was little real need for it. Seaplanes, on the other hand, were too cumbersome to operate effectively with the fleet at sea.

It was the latter problem that was the more important because its nature and the attempts to deal with it were to be at the heart of the development of carrier aviation. This, arguably, represented one of the three most significant developments in naval history. The problem centred on the fact that to be launched and recovered seaplanes had to use the surface of the sea, and this proved inimical to effective fleet operations. Seaplanes had to be winched by their parent ship on to and off the sea, and could only take off and land in a flat calm. Even then seaplanes were so underpowered and prone to mechanical failure that very often they could not take to the air at all. On Christmas Day 1914, for example, nine British seaplanes from the carriers *Empress*, *Engadine* and *Riviera* were committed to an attack on the Zeppelin base at Cuxhaven, but two failed to lift off. The raid was abortive, but it was the first ship-borne air strike in history, a glimpse of the future since this was a deliberate attempt to project offensive firepower into an enemy-controlled sea area where friendly surface ships dared not venture. Almost certainly the full implications of the attack were not realised at the time since the attack was also an attempt to project firepower into waters beyond the horizon. This represented a distinct qualitative change in naval warfare.

But in any sort of sea seaplanes could not operate, and the same was true of seaplane carriers themselves. The time they lost in launching and recovering their charges inevitably meant that they could not keep pace with a fast-moving fleet, and the first seaplane carriers were all converted merchantmen whose low speed in any case meant that they were ill-suited to meet the requirements of a fleet action. There had to be some purpose-built ship for operating flying machines at sea, but this was not very clear at the time. The concept of a ship that could fly-off or recover aircraft directly on to its deck(s) took a long time to be accepted, even though as early as 1910 the US Navy successfully flew an aircraft from the *Birmingham* and the following year recovered an aircraft on an improvised ramp erected on the *Pennsylvania*. The Americans, for some reason, did not persist with these trials which never involved ships that were under way.

Inevitably it was the British, since their need was the greatest, who led the move away from seaplane carriers in the direction indicated by the American experiments. In August 1915 the converted ex-Cunarder *Campania* flew off from her forward deck a wheeled seaplane while steaming at 17 knots. This represented a solution to half the problem, and it was a major significant advance. For the first time it became possible to launch aircraft without regard to sea conditions, and thus theoretically aircraft could hope to provide air cover and even a reconnaissance and strike capability for the fleet at sea. The catch, however, was that there was no means of recovery except by landing on the sea, and two years were to elapse before the British grasped this particular nettle with landing-on experiments with the *Furious*.

The *Furious* began life as a battlecruiser but before completion was converted to carry a forward launching platform complete with slotted rails to take the wheeled trolleys that had launched seaplanes from the *Campania*. She carried ten aircraft, six Sopwith Pup fighters that were tasked to tackle Zeppelins and four seaplanes. Because of the importance attached to the destruction of German airships the loss of a Pup on a one-way mission was acceptable, but in August 1917 the first attempt was made to land on the forward deck with one of the fighters. Despite the perils of having to skirt around the bridge and funnel the pilot managed to squeeze his aircraft on to the deck where it was grabbed and brought to a halt by crew members, but a second attempt to repeat this manoeuvre cost the pilot his life when a tyre burst on landing and the aircraft slewed over the side. This subsequently led to the further modification of the *Furious,* her rear turret being removed to provide a flying-on deck. This, however, was not a satisfactory arrangement because turbulence from bridge and funnel still made landing an unreasonably hazardous affair, and only three aircraft successfully carried out this feat. In order to minimise the risk of an aircraft ploughing into the funnel a strong rope net was erected at the end of the flying-on deck because initial experiments with arrester wires and undercarriage hooks proved insufficient to bring aircraft to a halt. Most aircraft trying to land on the *Furious* were written off in the attempt.

The metamorphosis of the *Furious* had but one stage to complete before she emerged as a recognisable carrier, and this was the displacement of bridge and funnel to provide a clear flight deck that could launch and recover aircraft. This was provided with the Argus which, with twenty aircraft, joined the fleet in October 1918 too late to see active service in the war. The island structure, offset to starboard, appeared in a British carrier in 1923 with the *Eagle* though her appearance was slightly overshadowed by the appearance of the first purpose-built carrier in December 1922. Whereas it might reasonably be supposed that such a ship, designed and built from the hull up as a carrier, would be if not British then American or French, in fact she was Japanese. The *Hosho* served notice to the rest of the world that science and technology were not subjects for which white nations had a patent.

The development of the *Furious* and *Argus,* nevertheless, represented a formidable advance in naval aviation, even though at the end of the war the *Furious* had been downgraded to a balloon ship. She raised carriers from the level of converted colliers, of which the *Ark Royal* had been one, to the dignity of a warship, even if her pedigree was dubious. She was a fleet unit capable of operating aircraft at the speed of the fleet or catching up if she was delayed. With 94,00-h.p. she had a top speed of 32 knots, almost three times that of the *Ark Royal* and the same as the heaviest battlecruisers then in service with the Royal Navy. She represented a remarkable achievement in what had been a war that had seen many remarkable achievements, and not a few set-backs, for naval aviation.

The war, naturally and inevitably, produced a host of 'firsts' for naval aviation. In the Baltic the Germans and Russians exchanged mines by aircraft, while at the Dardanelles in 1915 naval aircraft from the seaplane carrier *Ben-my-Chree* registered the first successful aerial torpedo strike with the damaging of a grounded freighter and then the damaging by torpedo attack of a ship with sea room and the power of manoeuvre. The first warship to be sunk by bombing, an otherwise insignificant wooden auxiliary minesweeper-guard ship, fell to the Japanese at Tsingtao, while the Germans claimed the first successful bombing of a capital ship when they severely damaged a Russian pre-dreadnought in April 1916. At Jutland a seaplane operated with the British fleet although it failed to have any impact on the battle. On various occasions ships had to defend themselves against air attack, and occasionally shot down their attackers. At the Dardanelles naval aircraft spotted for guns against short targets, and had it not been for their effectiveness many targets simply would never have been engaged. In this there was something of immense importance because controlled and effective fire against inland targets became possible for the first time. Yet even this seems relatively minor when set alongside a little known incident that took place on 25 April 1915 during the main force landings at Gallipoli. On that day seaplanes from the *Ark Royal* discovered a Turkish battleship, the *Turgud Reis,* firing from the Sea of Marmara across the Gallipoli peninsula against the Australian landing beaches. Their reports brought the battleship *Triumph* into action against the Turkish ship, her fire being directed across the intervening land mass by a kite-balloon operated by the *Manica.* It was the first time that a warship engaged another which was not in direct sight, and this was made possible by the development of air power. It was not important that the *Triumph* failed to hit the *Turgud Reis,* though the Turkish ship prudently withdrew, nor was it important that aircraft were not directly

76

or even indirectly concerned with the actual engagement. The significance of this incident was that the Sea of Marmara was firmly barred to British warships, except submarines, and there was no way in which British ships could function inside and beyond the Dardanelles. The *Triumph*'s action marked the first time when fire was directed beyond the horizon into enemy-controlled waters against a surface target, and it was only a matter of time before such a function fell to aircraft themselves. The Christmas Day raid on Cuxhaven had pointed firmly in this direction, and the *Ben-my-Chree*'s aircraft were to confirm this the following August.

The offensive use of aircraft at sea to project striking power into otherwise enemy-dominated areas was to be their proper and effective role, but it was precisely this role that, with certain limited exceptions, aircraft were denied during and after the First World War. Partly because of their limited numbers and capabilities aircraft and seaplanes were considered primarily in defensive terms. The British, for example, husbanded their fighters very carefully because they could be used only once. Fighters were held back to deal with Zeppelins; seaplanes were held back for reconnaissance once contact had been obtained by scouting light cruisers and not before. With their limited range, reporting facilities and launching opportunities they could not undertake aggressive reconnaissance, and they were not thought of in terms of spotting for guns during a fleet action. Kite-balloons, which extended the range of vision, were considered far more reliable and satisfactory for this task. With very few aircraft with the fleet - though this situation improved as aircraft were allotted to battleships and cruisers - there was very little scope for aircraft to operate offensively. Only when the *Argus* appeared was there any possibility of conducting more or less continuous air operations, but even her restricted number of aircraft, though a great advance on previous carriers, really limited her aircraft to a defensive role. Twenty aircraft were far too few to mount constant combat air patrol, still less to detach strength for offensive operations over an extended distance.

While carriers and aircraft alike continued to show considerable technical advances in the inter-war period, navies generally failed to consider carrier aviation in other than defensive terms. When it came to devising tactical doctrine, navies remained wedded to the conviction that the gun remained the most important weapon at sea. Concessions had to be made to the possibility of increasingly effective air attack, and these concessions took the form of thicker deck-armour, the fitting of anti-torpedo bulges, improved damage-control arrangements and the provision of ever more numerous dual-purpose and anti-aircraft weapons. But the general feeling in navies was that a properly handled battleship with sea room had cause to fear nothing but another battleship. Though the great fleets of the First World War had gone and no nation had the number of battleships that could be compared with the array of strength that had been marshalled in the North Sea between 1914 and 1918, the sanctity of the battle line remained. The battleship was still regarded as the arbiter of sea warfare, and all nations in the inter-war period continued to regard the battleship as the yardstick by which naval power was measured.

With all the advantages of hindsight it is easy to be critical of what appears to be crass stupidity and blindness, but at that time all navies had to feel their way in unknown territories, and they had to do so amid frenzied and fiercely partisan arguments that were waged between the aircraft's advocates and its detractors. On the one side were such commanders as the American General Mitchell whose fanatical promotion of air power so warped both his technical and political judgement that he brought himself to a court martial for his gross insubordination to authorities he considered to be less perceptive than himself. Mitchell argued that aircraft could sink warships and that all surface ships had been made obsolete by the advances that had been made and would be made in aviation. He secured his way in being allowed to carry out bombing trials against surrendered German warships in 1921. In these trials he was supposed to observe pauses between attacks in order to allow damage control parties to board the targets and assess the results. He simply ignored the rules and kept bombing the battleship *Ostfriesland* until she sank. Of course this proved nothing other than that a stationary hulk would sink if bombed long enough. Whether it was harder or easier to sink a hulk than a fighting ship depended on one's point of view, and the detractors of air power simply scorned the *Ostfriesland* affair as meaningless. In the very narrow sense they were quite correct. In a wider sense, of course, the *Ostfriesland* trial did show that a contemporary dreadnought was not invulnerable to air power, with the rider that the pace of future aircraft development was certain to outstrip the pace of development of means of defence. The caution of the vast majority of naval officers and the slowness of the evolution of tactical doctrine must be seen in the context of the bitter, and occasionally lunatic, argument over the relative merits of gun and aircraft that affected every major navy in the inter-war period. Most naval officers tried to steer a middle course between the two raging factions, and they were naturally loathe to abandon a proved weapon in favour of a weapon of unproven worth. For all navies there was always the restricting factor that to switch resources to naval aviation at the expense of the gun would be fatal if the aircraft failed to live up to the expectations of its advocates. It was this consideration that was the deciding factor in every major navy in the world building battleships in the years immediately before the Second World War.

Given this general caution it is not surprising that carrier aircraft were considered primarily as a means of defending the battle line. The main function of carrier aircraft was to fight for and secure air supremacy over the battleships and to defend them from enemy air attack. Second to this function was the spotting for the guns of the fleet, the aircraft being seen as an extension of the gun and as a means of enhancing its effectiveness. Subordinate to these tasks was the appreciation that attacks on an enemy in flight or out of range could be carried out in an attempt to bring about a fleet engagement that might otherwise never take place, just as the British did at Matapan in 1941 when three Italian heavy cruisers and two destroyers were destroyed in a surface action after a successful carrier strike from the *Formidable*. But all these tasks, along with a deep reconnaissance role that became possible as aircraft improved in range, speed and reliability, merely reflected the cautious view that missed the significance of the development of a weapons system (the carrier) that had no power in its own right but had value only in projecting firepower forward. It made no sense to define the tasks of carriers in defensive terms, but almost all of even the enthusiasts of air power missed this point. Radical elements thought in terms of fighting and winning the air battle before battle between surface units was joined. There was a growing feeling in some quarters that such an air battle, fought out of sight of both fleets, could well decide the outcome of any subsequent engagement. But very few followed this line of logic through to its conclusion. If indeed this was the case then battles over the battle line were irrelevant since the natural target of carrier aircraft had to be enemy carriers. These had to be singled out for destruction as the pre-requisite for success, and naturally it followed from this that the use of air power against an enemy line represented a gross misuse of offensive power. Of course this line of reasoning tipped over into the wider gun/aircraft controversy, but it is worth noting that Yamamoto, generally regarded as one of the most advanced thinkers of naval aviation matters in any navy, when he first conceived the idea of an attack on Pearl Harbor considered the prime target to be American battleships, not carriers. It was one of his most able staff officers, Genda, who alerted Yamamoto to the inconsistency of this approach and directed attention to taking out American carriers rather than the battleships.

There were technical problems which hampered the ability of carriers to operate in effective harness with battle fleets. For almost all the inter-war period battleships and carriers could not work side by side because of speed differential and the special requirements of the carrier for searoom, and they had to compete with one another for the allocation of escorts that were in desperately short supply in all navies at that time. These mundane problems were very real. Carriers were capable of operating at speeds up to 34 knots. They needed high speed in order to secure high wind speed across their decks for launching and recovering aircraft: Battleships, on the other hand, were slow, the *Queen Elizabeth*-class of 24/25 knots being amongst the fastest in the world. Until naval limitation treaties lapsed in 1936, therefore, and navies were left free to increase battleship size and incorporate in them new, lighter and more powerful boilers and engines, to try to put battleships and carriers in harness was an impossible task. The answer to this problem was provided by the Americans with the fast battleships of the *North Carolina* class: as long as a battleship could keep pace with a carrier then its massed batteries could provide protection for the carrier against a surface enemy, or more relevantly, air attack. Carriers with their clear flight decks often sought the comforting re-assurance of the guns of battleships and cruisers since their own defensive firepower was so relatively small.

The development of carrier warfare was not advanced very much by the outbreak of the European war in 1939 because of the peculiar circumstances of the naval war. The main factors in this state of affairs were that only one of the major combatants, Britain, operated carriers that had relatively few opportunities to operate offensively against enemy targets; and that British ideas, techniques, tactics and materièl were dated and British carriers were very poorly organised - the British lost one fleet carrier whilst it was conducting anti-submarine sweeps and another to the guns of battle units. The impact of carrier air power in the European context was lessened by the fact that it, and naval power generally, had to operate against a continental enemy that had all the advantages of good internal lines of communication by land and air within the continental land mass. In these circumstances carrier aviation could not hope to have as dramatic an impact, as for example, American and Japanese carriers might expect to achieve in a naval theatre of operations. Moreover, given the restricted waters in which British carriers had to operate on many occasions, particularly in the Mediterranean in the first half of the war, carrier aviation was always very vulnerable to enemy air power that could be concentrated far more quickly than naval forces could be assembled along external lines of communication. No instances show to better effect the problems presented to naval operations in this respect than the events off Greece and Crete in the spring of 1941. The British lost 22 warships and five transports sunk and a further fourteen ships damaged as a result of their being forced to operate in waters where British carriers could not hope to prove effective in the face of overwhelming shore-based enemy air supremacy. But once the tide of war changed and German air power was broken, as it was after 1943 when only 15 per cent of German air strength was left in southern Europe while about 70 per cent was in Germany itself, then allied naval power was successful in tying down between 5 per cent and 10 per cent of the German Army in defence of a long coastline that was wide open to attack. In this instance the threat of landings was, arguably, more potent than landings themselves.

These considerations, however, should not obscure the simple fact that while British carriers did enjoy successes, they were inadequately organised for the purposes of offensive operations. This situation persisted for most of the war. The most pertinent example of the limitations of British tactical thought, organisation and technique is the one action that is generally regarded as the crowning achievement of British carriers in a war where few chances of success came their way. This action was the *Bismarck* chase of 18-27 May 1941.

The *Bismarck* was the pride of the Kriegsmarine. Displacing 52,600 tons and with eight 15-in guns and a speed of 30.8 knots, she was more than equal to any battleship in service in the world at that time, and her commitment as a raider in the Atlantic in May 1941 was such a threat to British lines of communication that her destruction was an absolute priority to the British. Her departure from Norwegian waters in the company of the heavy cruiser *Prinz Eugen* was quickly known to the British whose heavy cruisers found the Germans as they broke into the Denmark Strait. To meet the raiders the British Home Fleet deployed its own pride, the *Hood,* and its newest battleship, the *Prince of Wales,* in a position to intercept the *Bismarck,* but in a singularly badly-fought action on the British part on 24 May the German ships blew the *Hood* out of the water with the loss of all but three of her crew of over 1,700 officers and men. The *Prince of Wales* was subjected to punishing attack before she broke off the action under cover of smoke, but had the Germans showed any initiative they would have forced the action until she had been despatched as well.

Three days were to separate the sinkings of the *Hood* and *Bismarck,* but in those three days the *Bismarck* almost managed to escape to the safety of Brest where the battlecruisers *Scharnhorst* and *Gneisenau* awaited her after their own successful raiding operations. The *Bismarck* survived a carrier strike from the *Victorious* with one hit on her armoured belt that did no damage, and she managed to shake off shadowing British cruisers to break free of the net of nineteen British carriers, battleships and cruisers that attempted to close in on her. The speed and course of the *Bismarck* ensured her safety until the 26th when she was found by a Catalina reconnaissance aircraft from RAF Coastal Command. Thereafter the only threat to her came from Force H, coming up from Gibraltar after an operation to fly aircraft into Malta. With no chance of the British ships astern of the *Bismarck* bringing the German ship to action unless she was first slowed, aircraft from the *Ark Royal,* launched in wild weather, crippled the *Bismarck* with a torpedo that smashed the steering gear and jammed the rudder to port.

Attacked throughout the night by British destroyers, the next morning the *Bismarck* was the almost unmanoeuvrable recipient of the attentions of the battleships *Rodney* and *King George V.* The two British battleships reduced the *Bismarck* to a shambles before scuttling charges and torpedoes finally sent the German ship to the bottom. Neither her armoured belt nor her boiler and engine rooms were pierced by British shells in the course of the action, and the British battleships only made contact by the dangerously narrow margin of three hours. Some British ships had less than five tons of oil left when they reached port.

The British appreciated the obvious lesson of the *Bismarck* chase. Had it not been for carrier aircraft from the *Ark Royal* the *Bismarck* would have reached the safety of a French port and there would have been absolutely nothing that the British surface ships could have done to prevent this happening. The fact that her belt remained intact showed that the *Bismarck* was more than capable of looking after herself in an action with a surface enemy. But the two real lessons of the action were very different, and these went largely unappreciated at the time. Firstly, surface raiders in the Atlantic were certain to be a declining force in the face of growing numbers of aircraft and the development of radar: the great successes of German raiders in 1940 and early 1941 were things of the past. Secondly, and here was the crux of the matter, it could be argued had the British not spread their carriers into mixed task forces in order to support battleships and had they concentrated all their carriers from the Home Fleet into a single strike force, then the likelihood is that the *Bismarck* would have been caught and destroyed - ideally in the Denmark Strait where the presence of the ice cap denied her room to manoeuvre - more quickly, more easily and without the loss of the *Hood.* There would have been no need for surface ships to tackle so formidable an adversary as the *Bismarck,* and certainly not when she was at full fighting effectiveness. As it was a grand total of 48 warships were involved in hunting the *Bismarck* and the action and success of the *Ark Royal* were quite fortuitous. The chances of a handful of obsolete torpedo-planes crippling the *Bismarck* in a single strike were exceedingly remote, but there would have been reasonable odds of inflicting appreciable and perhaps crippling damage if all the aircraft from Britain's available carriers had been concentrated for one massed attack in the waters that separate Greenland from Iceland. It would have made better sense to have used surface ships against the *Bismarck* only in the event of aircraft failing rather than before they were used.

Events in the South China Sea on the following 10 December showed that one navy appreciated the lessons that aircraft, in this case long-range shore-based naval aircraft, could deal with enemy capital ships far more effectively and economically that could surface units. On that day the *Repulse* became the first capital ship to be sunk on the open sea by aircraft, her companion, the *Prince of Wales,* also succumbing to an overwhelming air attack that cost the Japanese just three of the 88 aircraft thrown against the British force.

The Japanese success on this occasion was deliberately and carefully earned, and thoroughly merited, and there was no element of good fortune about it even though the British could consider themselves unlucky to have been discovered by the extreme flanking aircraft in a line of searchers that were at the very end of their endurance. But the important aspect of the events of 10 December 1941 is that it formed part of a series of amphibious offensives behind a front secured by aircraft, in this case shore-based aircraft in the absence of otherwise-engaged carriers. The Japanese counter to the arrival of the British force in the Far East, given the commitment of the carrier force to the Pearl Harbor attack, was to reinforce the XXIInd Air Flotilla in southern Indo-China with long-range strike aircraft. This they chose to do instead of reinforcing the already-strong Southern Force with any of the six battleships held in the strategic reserve in Japanese home waters. In Japanese concepts of war the holding back and preservation of main battle units for political purposes and to meet some supreme crisis or need for 'the decisive battle' was paramount, and it formed a central part of Japanese strategy right up until the destruction of Japanese naval power at the Battle of the Philippine Sea in June 1944.

In the first five months of the Pacific war, when Japanese forces reduced allied resistance in Malaya, The Philippines and the Indies, Japanese concepts worked well enough, the campaign in the Indies being an impressive example of Japanese economy of effort in developing a series of offensives against tactical objectives behind a front secured by air power. In this process land-based naval and military aircraft and aircraft from the carriers complemented one another as Japanese forces broke through the Bangka Strait, the Makassar Strait and the Molucca Passage to bring about the rupture of allied strength along the Malay

Barrier. In this series of events the Japanese used their air power offensively to fight for and secure air supremacy over their objectives before the arrival of amphibious forces, and to carry out a series of attacks designed to cripple any allied response before a counter-move could become effective. In this process Japanese carriers took station on the left, holding the open Pacific flank, though they pushed through the Banda and Flores Seas to strike at Darwin, a strategic target on account of its being a staging post for reinforcements and supplies being sent to the Indies. Later Japanese carrier forces moved into the Indian Ocean to participate in the annihilation of allied shipping fleeing from a doomed Java.

In the course of little more than four months Japanese carriers, always operating at least in pairs and normally in groups of four, five or six, conducted operations that ranged over half the circumference of the globe. From Hawaii in the east to Ceylon in the west Japanese carriers carried out a series of operations that perhaps made them the most destructive naval force in history. They numbered amongst their many victims five American battleships and two British heavy cruisers and a light carrier. Yet notwithstanding their success, strategic results eluded them. At Pearl Harbor the Japanese were unfortunate enough to find the base empty of the Pacific Fleet's three carriers, while in the Indies and the Indian Ocean Japanese tactical victories were registered against enemies already beaten or possibly irrelevant to the outcome of the war. Japan, in the spring of 1942, was in the position of having to consolidate her gains, and this she could do only by registering decisive strategic success. To achieve this she attempted to force an action in the central Pacific with the Pacific Fleet in an effort to destroy American carrier forces before they became too powerful to challenge. The course of subsequent events, namely the rough handling Japanese carriers received at the Coral Sea in May and the disaster they encountered at Midway in June, is so well known to need no further elaboration other than to observe that perhaps the Japanese might have been better served had they chosen to make their effort in other directions against strategic targets no less important for their not being American carriers. One obvious target for such an effort may well have been the Persian Gulf. At Easter 1942 Japanese carriers raided Ceylon in the hope of catching the British fleet that had been hastily assembled in the Indian Ocean. It was a very poorly judged move strategically since a single sortie had no real hope of bringing to battle a force that in terms of fighting power could not influence the outcome of the war. The lack of depth and time allowed in the carriers, and their subsequent inability to maintain a high tempo of sustained operations, ensured that there could not be an attack against any strategic

84

target either important in its own right or sufficiently important to force the British to give battle on unequal terms. But, instead of a short duration raid, a major sustained effort against the Gulf via Ceylon (India being left to fall to pieces *en passant*) *may* well have forced Britain out of the war, with incalculable results stemming from the draining of much of American strength out of the Pacific and into the Atlantic. Of course all kinds of problems of logistics, time, distance and space are involved in the consideration of this *if*, but there was very little damage that the Americans could have done to Japanese positions in the Pacific at this time and there was certainly very little of substance with which the British could have opposed any assault on the Gulf. Perhaps the speculation is fanciful and conditioned by the thought that anything would have been an improvement on what the Japanese attempted to do with such disastrous results in 1942. But as an idea it serves to illustrate that non-military factors such as geographical position, access to resources, time, distance and space are as potent factors in strategic deliberation as force itself.

The Japanese, in the opening months of the Pacific war, showed that they had absorbed many of the technical and tactic aspects of carrier operations. But Midway was to show that they had neglected the problem of fighting their carriers defensively while their characteristic dispersal of force during the approach to contact phase resulted in their task groups being caught and defeated without their being able either to offer one another mutual protection or to counter-attack effectively. But though there were these elements of tactical and technical failure on the part of the Imperial Navy, the prime Japanese failure was strategic. Their failure resulted from getting themselves into a position where they felt they had no option but to go to war with a nation which at the war's end mustered sixteen fleet carriers, with another thirteen building, eight light fleet carriers, with two more under construction, and no less than 64 escort carriers, twenty more having been launched and in the process of completion. Such was the strength available to the Americans that the weakest of the three carrier task group that fought at the Philippine Sea was, with a mere (*sic*) two fleet carriers, two light fleet carriers, two battleships, one anti-aircraft and three heavy cruisers and eighteen destroyers, no weaker than the entire American fleet at Midway. When these strengths are put alongside comparative aircraft production the full extent of Japanese strategic folly can be appreciated. Total Japanese aircraft production from 1941 until the end of the war is estimated to have been 69,888 of which 30,447 were fighters. The Navy's best fighter, the A6M Zero-sen numbered 10,449. American aircraft production stood at 49,445 in 1942 alone and doubled by 1944. Corsairs, Hellcats, Thunderbolts and Mustangs each out-numbered the Zero-sen, the Lightning only narrowly failing to do so. Not even the demands of the European theatre could siphon off American strength to the extent that Japanese hopes of a negotiated peace would become reasonable.

When this awesome level of production was blended with ever-growing skill and technique in all aspects of naval operations, the result had to be overwhelming victory. The Americans had their bad moments, particularly in 1942 when they were for a time reduced to one operational carrier in the whole of the Pacific. Midway was followed by a series of battles in the Solomons that cost the Americans dearly, but the American and Japanese losses balanced one another. This, in strategic terms, con-stituted American victory because Japanese losses were inflicted on a Navy that was at the peak of its strength and lacked the ability to make good its losses whereas American losses were quickly made good by the upsurge in American production. Yet perhaps the most impressive aspect of the American effort in the Pacific was not in the handling, strength and sheer fighting professionalism of the US Navy but in the manner in which it converted itself from a 'short-haul' to a 'long-haul' navy in the course of hostilities.

Perhaps no other aspect of naval development in these years com-pares to this change. Certainly the development of carrier aviation did not alter basic concepts of war beyond certain limits, critically important though these were. The range of action was extended over the horizon and this, as mentioned earlier, represented a dramatic and fundamental change in the conduct of operations. The development of fast carrier task forces allowed overwhelming concentration of force to be achieved against individual targets before an enemy had the chance to counter-attack, as the preliminary exchanges at the Battle of the Philippine Sea showed only too well. Through surprise and concentration the Americans annihilated Japanese land-based air power in the Marianas before the main action was joined, the Americans thus being able to destroy Japanese forces piecemeal before they could concentrate. American carrier strength allowed the Americans to fight in strength whereas the Japanese were forced to fight from a position of marked and increasing inferiority the longer the battle lasted. Carrier aviation, moreover, could supplement strategic bombing, by flying combat air patrols not over the carriers themselves but over enemy airfields. This the Americans called 'The Big Blue Blanket', first used in the assault on Mindoro when fleet carriers flew a total of 1,671 sorties against Japanese airfields on Luzon, 1,427 of them by fighters. The same tactic was repeated in the last stages of the war against Japan herself. But when all these elements are associated with an ability of ships to stay at sea for

'The Capture of the *Gloriosa*', by C Brooking (1747).

HMS *Lion* hit on 'Q' turret at Jutland, 1916.

The Grand Fleet patrolling in the North Sea.

The *Seydlitz* burning at Jutland.

The Japanese battleship *Yamato,* December 1941. She was sunk at the battle of Okinawa, 1945.

opposite: Japanese ships scatter to evade a raid by aircraft from USS *Saratoga* on Rabaul harbour, November 1943.

HMS *Sheffield* in heavy seas on Arctic convoy escort duty, 1943.

top: German U-boat *U25* type 1A, 740 tons.

centre: Russian Delta class ballistic missile submarine.

below: A Whisky class submarine of the Soviet navy on patrol in the North Atlantic. Based on the design of surrendered German U-boats, this class was produced in large numbers.

left: The Russian battle cruiser *Kirov,* the biggest warship, apart from aircraft carriers, to be built for more than thirty years.

below: The Soviet warship *Kiev,* a 43,000-ton CVS with a 35-strong air group.

HMS *Invincible* shown launching a Sea Harrier from her 6½-degree angled flight deck.

The nuclear-powered Attack Aircraft Carrier USS *Enterprise*. The largest warship ever built at the time of her construction (1958-60). She is currently being refitted. She has an air group of 84 aircraft.

months at a time, to carry out all but the most major and serious repairs without returning to a fleet base and to simply 'live off its tail' in terms of supplies, fuel, ordnance and manpower reserves, the extent of flexibility conferred on task forces by the development of the fleet train can be appreciated.

Before 1941 the conventional wisdom of the day was that fleets lost 10 per cent of their effectiveness for every 1,000 miles they steamed from their bases. Effective fighting ranges for fleets were reckoned to be no more than 2,000 miles. But a little more than 1,800 miles and six months separated the American landings on Tarawa and Saipan. The Battle of the Philippine Sea and the landings in the Marianas were conducted by American forces some sixty degrees of longtitude west of their main fleet base at Pearl Harbor while MacArthur's main thrust along the northern New Guinea coast and into The Philippines was even further from Hawaii. Deserted and hitherto unknown atolls such as Manus and Ulithi were transformed into complete fleet bases with every facility as the Americans carried the war into Japanese-conquered areas. In the combat zone itself literally hundreds of ubiquitous repair ships, salvage vessels and tugs were on hand to succour damaged ships. Statistics almost become meaningless in trying to convey the sheer size of the American effort, but when it is realised that at the end of the war the US Navy had a total of about 78,000 vessels of all types, ranging from the mightiest of warships through the assault craft to the most humble of auxiliaries, then the sheer cost, extent and meaning of oceanic sea power can begin to be appreciated. Attention is always fixed upon the big ships or the assault craft, but no fewer than 104 fast oilers, 32 base tankers, 39 store ships, 94 fast and 178 slow cargo ships and 192 fast and another 135 slow transports formed just a small part of the support ships that ranged from docks to hospital ships to survey vessels. It was this tail of support, enabling the Americans to strike with massive power for long periods of time without having to return to base, that put the US Navy in a class of its own. The Royal Navy, with six fleet and four light fleet carriers and 38 escort carriers in commission at the end of the war, was a pygmy in comparison, yet it was by far the second most powerful oceanic navy in the world and it was the only navy that could realistically stand comparison with the US Navy. It was this massive flexibility and strike power on the part of the Americans that has so excited Soviet envy and admiration in the post-war world, even though the Soviets have consistently belittled the importance of sea power in deciding the outcome of the Second World War.

Within the American framework of operations the escort carriers played a vital part though they were inevitably overshadowed by the larger and more photogenic fleet carriers. Yet it is perhaps a curious fact that the largest of the fleet carriers, the 11,400-ton *Sangamon* class, were bigger than the nine 11,000-ton *Independence* class light fleet carriers. In the number of aircraft carried there was little to choose between the two classes, but the difference between attack carriers and the normal escort carriers was very marked. The original ten-strong *Essex*-class carriers each deployed about 100 aircraft on 27,100 tons. They had a speed of some 33 knots. A typical member of the *Bogue* escort class, eleven of which entered American service while another 26 experienced British employment, displaced 9,800 tons and with a speed of 18 knots had a complement of 21 aircraft. Escort carriers carried a crew one quarter the size of that of a large fleet carrier. The vital part played by escort carriers in the Pacific war was in the close support of landings, the ferrying of aircraft reinforcements to fleet carriers and shore establishments from rear base areas and, in a few urgent cases, as substitutes for fleet carriers. Because of their low speed and relativly few aircraft they were never more than a rather unsatisfactory stop-gap in this latter capacity. They also served in an anti-submarine role, and it was for this task that such ships had been originally conceived. The British desire to provide convoys with continuous air cover, particularly important in 1940 and 1941 until Luftwaffe bomber strength was siphoned off to eastern Europe, prompted the commissioning of a small carrier, bereft of sophistication, that carried a handful of Martlet fighters. This first escort carrier, the *Audacity,* was British, though more accurately not much more than the flight deck was British: the rest had been unwittingly supplied by the Germans in the form of a prize, the *Hannover*. She had no island and no elevator, and her six aircraft had to be lashed to the deck when not flying. She was lost on her first operational mission, the defence of convoy HG 76 from Gibraltar to Britain in December 1941, but not before she demonstrated the potential of such ships. Her aircraft accounted for two German bombers and helped in the destruction of five submarines. The U-boats in return sank two merchantmen, a destroyer and the *Audacity*. Simply on the balance of losses the convoy constituted a substantial British success, notwithstanding the loss of the carrier, but it was very significant in one other way. The Gibralter-Britain route was one of the most hazardous for British shipping because it ran across the face of German air and submarine bases in western France, and against the 32-strong convoy the Germans directed more than twenty U-boats. Given the size of the attacker's strength the loss of just two merchantmen was a very good outcome and an indication of what a strong and well-trained escort could achieve when it had the support of integrated air power.

Subsequent escort carriers showed significant qualitative improvements over the *Audacity* (they could hardly have done otherwise) though it was not until April 1943 that the first purpose-built escort carrier, the 7,800-ton *Casablanca* (28 aircraft, 19 knots), was launched by the Americans. But though such ships could operate far more efficiently than converted ships, they could not perform any different tasks. Their main role in the defence of convoys was reconnaissance, particularly at first and last light when an unwary, unlucky or persistent U-boat might be caught on the surface either withdrawing from or advancing to contact. The offensive capability of aircraft from escort carriers was very limited, but their value lay in being able to force down a U-boat or direct surface escorts to its location in order to attempt its destruction. Aircraft were particularly useful in covering the area astern of a convoy where the escorts were invariably weak, and in forcing down reporting U-boats, thereby breaking contact between the hunter and the hunted and in fact reversing the roles.

The escort carrier thus played a very important part in reversing the tide of battle. Escort carriers allowed convoys to control more effectively the seas through which they passed by adding to the effectiveness and range of escorts that were already undergoing considerable qualitative improvements through the acquisition of radar (thus depriving the U-boats of its invisibility as it closed a convoy), direction finders (for fixing the location of transmitting submarines) and new weapons. Escort carriers also made their contribution to the process by which those areas of sea not previously covered by allied aircraft, where U-boats could run on the surface and recharge their batteries in safety, were gradually closed. The acquisition of bases in Iceland and the Azores and the use of Very Long Range Aircraft were vital in this process, and it must be recalled that shore-based aircraft proved far more effective as U-boat killers than aircraft from ships. As mentioned earlier, 245 U-boats were destroyed by shore-based aircraft and two more were shared with ship-borne aircraft: the latter accounted for 43 submarines. The importance of the substantial contribution made by ship-borne aircraft to the defeat of the U-boats - which was so often defensive and negative with no 'kill' to show at the end - must be seen within the context of an overall battle to retain command of the sea and not just for control of the sea around a convoy at any one point in time.

Naval aviation came of age in the course of the Second World War, the Americans and to a lesser extent the Japanese being the pioneers of new tactical concepts that changed the face, but not the substance, of naval warfare. The significance of developments in naval aviation was not that they changed strategic concepts but that they affected the manner in which action was fought and profoundly altered the balance between different types of ship. By the end of the war surface ships could not hope to operate in their own right. They could not hope to operate and survive unless they did so in waters where air superiority already existed or in the company of carriers that were prepared to fight for and secure command of the air. In these circumstances surface ships still had an enormously important role to play in providing fire support for landings and for carriers, but their role was clearly circumscribed by the rise to pre-eminence of a weapons system whose effectiveness reached some ten times beyond the range of the largest naval gun.

There are two lessons that emerged from the war that we can mention in this context. First surface ships, without air support, imposed no check on a fleet based on the carrier. The second was scarcely less obvious, but could be missed. In an attempt to ward off defeat the Japanese had recourse to the one advantage they held over the allies throughout the war. This was their superior morale that was manifest in their willingness, indeed their eagerness, to die in the service of their emperor. The *kamikaze* tactics they employed used obsolescent aircraft and poorly trained pilots (who did not have to be taught to land) in the most effective manner possible. This was to crash their aircraft into allied warships, the American fleet carriers being singled out as the main targets. Initial surprise achieved some success and the sheer intensity of such raids inevitably produced results, most notably off Okinawa where no less than twenty American fleet destroyers were either sunk or damaged beyond repair. Many carriers were hit, seven of the *Essex*-class being damaged in varying degrees. But overall less than one in four suicide aircraft inflicted some form of damage and only one in 33 ever sank an enemy ship. No carrier was ever sunk by a kamikaze and the two most serious American fleet carrier casualties of 1944 and 1945, the *Princeton,* which was lost, and the *Franklin,* which miraculously survived, were both accounted for by conventional attack. The kamikaze experience showed that morale cannot make good too substantial a material deficit, in this case sailors who wanted to live being more than a match for pilots who died in order to fight. But it showed our second point: that there was no effective substitute for orthodox naval power and, in particular, there was no effective substitute for conventional naval air power. Whether in a fleet or trade protection role, air power had proved decisive, as long as it formed part of a balanced force that was built around it.

CHAPTER V

EVER MORE FOR EVER LESS:
THE RISE OF THE SOVIET NAVY

The end of the Second World War saw the passing of two elements that had been constant features of naval warfare for several hundred years. The first was that of British naval supremacy that had generally prevailed since the days of Cromwell. The second was that of the surface ship's period of dominance. The mantle of both had fallen upon the American aircraft carriers, a force so powerful that no navy could hope to stand against it.

These transitions were relatively painless for the British because they took place during a war when they and the Americans had been intimately associated as allies, and the smoothness of change, plus the totality of American power, ensured that there would not be any significant change in the role and functions of sea power. The only element of novelty lay in the fact that naval ships with Stars and Stripes rather than White Ensigns continued to function in the manner in which British warships had always functioned. Not even the advent of nuclear weapons had any real impact on naval strategy and tactics. The conventional wisdom of the day was that the sheer size and weight and the small number of nuclear weapons in existence in the decade after 1945 would preclude their use at sea. Ports, it was recognised, were likely to be targets for strategic nuclear attack, but the use of nuclear weapons against naval forces on the high seas was believed to be unrealistic. This is not the case today.

The navies of the world, in any case, had more than their hands full merely trying to meet the needs of peace. In some cases this meant putting ships into reserve and demobilising manpower: in other cases it meant the rebuilding of navies devastated by war. But all, irrespective of their condition, had to pay attention to clearing the debris of war. Mines had to be cleared and destroyed; one German minesweeping flotilla, the 22nd, remained operational under allied command as late as 1948 and several more were not disbanded until late 1947. Wrecks had to be charted and either marked or removed: salvage had to be attempted.

Men and material had to be moved to occupy former enemies or back home. Enemy troops had to be repatriated and civilian populations in many countries had to be fed because, for the moment, they could not provide for themselves. Such tasks, and those brought about by normal peaceful use of the sea, kept navies busy for several years trying to put right some of the damage they themselves had caused in more hazardous times.

Yet, inevitably, there could be no preserving the political, strategic and technical status quo as it existed in 1945, and even in their moment of triumph the Anglo-American navies could identify one obvious future problem. The totality of their victory did not obscure the unpleasant fact that in the last weeks of the war the Germans had put new and very fast submarines to sea. These, the Types XXI and XXIII, were capable of submerged speeds that enabled them to outstrip surface escorts. Given the fact that sonar performance fell away at high speed, escorts were forced to face problems in their anti-submarine operations that were certain to mount if and when nuclear power became adopted as the means of propulsion for submarines.

The search for antidotes to fast submarines was therefore a technical one, but technical requirements came to merge with political and strategic necessity in time because the onset of the Cold War produced for the Anglo-American navies a potential enemy whose main oceanic forces were submarines. This opponent was, of course, the Soviet Navy, the rise of which has been one of the most spectacular naval developments of modern time. From being a navy whose record in the Second World War was, to put it mildly, abysmal, and whose effectiveness in 1945 was negligible, the Soviet Navy in less than four decades has become almost as large as the American Navy. Morever, because of the consistency and sheer size of Soviet construction and the relatively small building programmes put in hand by western navies, it may well be that the Soviet advantage in lead-time is now such that within a decade the Soviet Navy will relegate the US navy to a position of decided inferiority. The US defence budget for FY 81 is to show a 50 per cent increase in weapons procurement alone - to $30,000,000,000 - but such an amount, half as much again as the entire British defence appropriations and double the Soviet Navy's budget, will do little in the short term to check the process whereby an ageing American fleet is faced by an ever growing modern Soviet fleet. The position of the lesser naval powers, Britain, France, Germany, Italy and Japan, is even more serious, of course.

The development of Soviet naval power, naturally, has been a conscious and deliberate one, initially prompted by Soviet naval inferiority to the Anglo-American fleets at the end of the war. The Anglo-American achievement at sea in the war had been in two immediate fields, those of carrier and amphibious operations, and at the war's end the Soviet Union was hopelessly vulnerable on both counts. She had no counter to either American carriers or the Anglo-American ability to mount amphibious operations in the manner that had been carried out in the Mediterranean, Normandy and in the Pacific.

The Soviet response to her position of inferiority was a reflection of several conflicting influences. Historically, Russia, under the Tsars, always had pretensions to be a sea power. From the time in the eighteenth century when Peter the Great pushed Russia's borders to the Sea of Azov and then to the Baltic with the founding in 1703 of St Petersburg, and later when Catherine the Great's Russia expanded southwards to include the Crimea and a secure footing on the Black Sea, sea power has been important to Russia. Russia's gains of Azov and during the Great Northern War (1700-1721) were in part secured by Russian naval victories over the Turks and Swedes. Navarino and Sinope were instances of Tsarist sea power having a major influence on European events, while a little known aspect of Commodore Perry's opening up of Japan to western influence in the 1850s was the fact that his first visit to Japan was paralleled by a visit of a Russian squadron from Europe. To Perry went the credit, or blame, of forcing Japan to open her doors to the west, but in reality it was the combination of American and Russian sea power, plus the certainty that the arrival of the British and French in strength would not long be delayed, that prompted Japan to start making concessions to the occidental powers.

But while sea power has been important to Russia, geography dictates that it could never be more than marginal in her strategic needs. Despite a 28,000 mile (43,000-km) coastline, all but 10 per cent of it icebound, Russia is largely land-locked with enormously long land frontiers on the other side of which in Europe were nations that were industrially and technically far superior to her. Russia's historic concern, therefore, has been primarily with ground forces. Sea power could never play a significant role for a country with very little seaborne trade and relatively few ports and cities that were vulnerable to sea-borne assault. Indeed, during the Crimean War (1854-1856) Anglo-French forces dominated all the seas that wash Russia with a totality that was unequalled, either before or since, but to no real effect or purpose. Anglo-French superiority at sea could not be translated into strategic gain because Russia could draw from within its own land mass for its needs, and she was more or less invulnerable to sea power with regard to her capacity to wage war. What gains the British and French made, and even they did not try to operate against the Kronshtadt naval base in the Gulf of Finland because it was far too strong to be assaulted, proved to be only temporary.

Navies for Russia were always a luxury, subordinate to military needs and demands, and any desire to acquire significant naval power had to take second place to the needs of security on land. Moreover, Russia's naval priorities always had to be divided into four, and possibly five, separate areas that were unable to offer one another mutual support. These areas were, and still remain, the Black, Baltic and White Seas and the Pacific, the Caspian being another area of interest though very much subordinate to the others. To add to this problem of diffusion of strength - which has tended to obscure the fact that generally over the last two centuries Russia has always been amongst the top six naval powers -was the simple fact that in the west the exits from her two most important sea areas, the Baltic and Black Seas, were directly under foreign control.

Russian naval policy vacillated traditionally between the desire to have a high seas capability and a caution that firmly pointed to her never going beyond coastal defence forces. Whether under the Tsars or Soviets lack of funds, skilled labour and building facilities, a shortage of trained naval personnel and the priority accorded land forces always served to dampen enthusiasm for oceanic forces. Historically, notwithstanding the relative lack of importance of the sea for Russia in either strategic or economic terms, there has been a persistent wish to acquire the power and prestige of the kind the Royal Navy bestowed upon Britain in her heyday - though this wish has been very difficult to rationalise. Modern Soviet naval writings have been plagued by the inconsistency between the assertion that sea power is vital but that the outcome of the Second World War was decided on land and the sea was only marginal to its result. Even Japan, according to Soviet versions of history, was defeated by the Soviet Army's operations in Manchuria after the Americans had fumbled opportunities in the Pacific for more than three years. Though this belittling of sea power was the obvious outcome of the political wish to downgrade American and British contributions to the defeat of the Axis powers, it leaves a basic flaw in Soviet naval thought since either sea power was important in the war, and hence the Soviet aspiration to secure sea power is only natural, or sea power was not - and Soviet aspirations are therefore unnecessary and wasteful.

But irrespective of the wish to secure sea power in a genuine deep-water sense the realities of geography and power have always, until the present time, confounded the attempt, but the inherent tensions within the political and defence hierarchies and within the navy between advocates of oceanic forces and their opponents was never more obvious than in Stalin's Soviet Union. Stalin himself had no knowledge or understanding of naval warfare, but he was a supporter of the idea of the Soviet Union securing a deep-water capability for political reasons. Yet in two different times, first before and then after the Second World War, he was unable to build up oceanic forces to match his aspirations. In both cases the major factor in this failure was the perennial problem of lack of funds and industrial strength, plus the fact that the Navy had to take a back seat to other, more urgent tasks. In both cases, moreover, time was against Stalin, in the first instance because of the Soviet Union's untimely involvement in war, on the second occasion because of his long-overdue demise.

The period before the Second World War (for the Soviets the Great Patriotic War of 1941-1945) was one of immense significance in the development of the Soviet Navy. It is also very important for any understanding of the place sea power holds in Soviet strategic thinking, but it is a period that is very difficult to unravel. Harrison Salisbury once made the comment that Soviet history books should have detachable pages to allow their easier rewriting to take account of who is in disgrace at any given time. Any examination of this period is bedevilled by this problem and by the tendency, prevalent in the Khrushchev era, to blame Stalin for any and all shortcomings and failures. The obscure semantics of ideological and defence debates, the lack of openness in Soviet government and the need to try to guess intentions from scraps of information and actual subsequent developments make the interpretation of Soviet naval policy difficult. Moreover, one is conditioned to consider policy in rational terms and to attempt to explain a course of events as a sequence of logical cause-effect relationships. In trying to find one's way through the tangled affairs of Soviet naval development, however, the element of the irrational is always present, and this is not simply a reflection of a peculiarity in the interpretation of history or merely the natural human failure to think things through logically. There is evidence of the illogical - the personal pecadilloes of Stalin and Khrushchev are obvious examples - and there is always the need to bear in mind that these events are subject to various interpretations. It would be altogether wrong to consider Soviet naval development either in wholly rational terms or by western norms.

What is clear, however, is that for the best part of a decade after 1922 the low priority assigned the Navy was in part a reflection of the poor political esteem in which it was held by the CPSU. While many factors can be considered to be important in producing this situation, three may be regarded as critical in bringing about this state of affairs. These are firstly the basic political and military stance of the infant USSR at this time; secondly, the industrial and financial weakness of the

Soviet economy; thirdly, the effects of the Kronshtadt mutiny and the general suspicion in which the Navy generally, its officers and its various schools of thought were held by the communist leadership.

Of these the first, the basic political and military philosophy of the USSR, was by far the most important. The new republic emerged from civil war and foreign intervention in support of the anti-Bolshevik forces with more than a mere suspicion that it was surrounded by enemies, who, given a renewed opportunity, would seek to destroy it. If there was an element of paranoia in this, then it is hardly surprising. What the Soviets had to do was to consolidate their land forces to ensure not merely their domestic authority but physical security against future invasion. Compared to this the needs of the Navy - and still less any thought of a blue-water fleet - were utterly irrelevant. Interventionist sea power, even in the Baltic and despite the successful British attack on Kronshtadt, had had no decisive impact on the outcome of the struggle for power in post-1917 Russia. Even when Soviet political and military thinking began to turn for the first time towards offensive notions, again the Navy had little cause for cheer. By the late 'twenties Soviet thought had begun to consider an offensive strategy involving the establishment of Soviet hegemony over Poland and Rumania, and this, by definition, would be a land and not a sea task. No sensible Bolshevik in this period could consider the Navy in terms other than its being a purely defensive force designed to ensure the security of the sea flanks of the Red Army.

The influence of other factors in Soviet naval development (or non-development) in the 'twenties, including the state of industry and the domestic naval situation, are less easy to explain, and equally hard to evaluate. It would seem that they were very much subordinate to the strategic posture of the USSR, and its alternating senses of security and insecurity. Given that the theme of this essay is concerned with notions of sea power, it is convenient and right to trace inter-war developments by reference to the internal state and the strategic thinking of the Soviet Navy. These elements, it must be remembered, were or seem to have been secondary to the wider strategic considerations of policy.

1922 is an appropriate year in which to begin with the narrative of the Soviet Navy because in that year members of the Baltic Fleet mutinied against the increasing authoritarianism of Lenin's rule. Their action, carried out by the élite Bolshevik force in the October 1917 revolution and during the civil war, discredited the Navy in the eyes of its political masters. The mass executions and deportations to Siberia that followed the mutiny's suppression did nothing to enhance the efficiency and professionalism of a force with none too distinguished a record at sea in both the First World War and the Intervention. The fact that many

Tsarist officers (i.e. politically unreliable class enemies) had to be retained in command appointments was a further factor in the suspicion in which the Navy was held, and their persistent support for oceanic concepts of sea power (the so-called Old School), totally beyond Soviet reach at that time, did little to endear them to a party that under Stalin after 1927 (i.e. the fall of Trotsky) increasingly sought to interpret naval strategy in narrowly ideological terms.

Initially the Old School was very powerful in the Navy. It believed that though submarines and aircraft made the fulfilment of its tasks more difficult, the battleship remained the most important weapons system afloat. The school stressed what was, in effect, an 'all-arms' concept of sea power, emphasising the need for balanced forces of all types of warships and aircraft, and it adhered to the concept of the unity and indivisibility of command of the sea. The school had to trim its sails to take account of the country's straightened circumstances, but it rejected the notion of the opposition Young School that battleships had lost their importance. It rejected, moreover, the idea that submarines could exercise sea power. Gervais, one of the most influential members of the Old School, argued with a clarity that would have been welcome to Wegener, Assmann and Döenitz, that a submarine guerre de course could be beaten, given sufficient resources being diverted to the proper provision of escorts. He argued that submarines could not discharge the equally important task of defending one's own lines of communication with the outside world. To men such as Gervais notions of local defence forces and sea denial could not prevail against the historical certainty of Mahanite concepts and the reality of balanced fleets in Britain, France, Japan and the USA.

Naval logic favoured Gervais and likeminded colleagues, but present reality and future fortune did not. The Old School was to be vindicated by the march of events, but not before its members had been purged, along with many of their opponents. The latter had been more realistic in the 'twenties and 'thirties, not that that saved them from the indiscriminate slaughter that Stalin unleashed at the end of the 'thirties. Their dismissal of the battleship was overstated, based as it was on a false reading of the moratorium on capital ship construction following the Washington Treaties (1921-1922) and by the failure to see the political significance of heavy surface units. But in this the Young School was not really any different from certain bodies of opinion in other navies. The school stressed the efficacy of light coastal forces for the defence of the Soviet Union, and such forces, unlike those sought by the Old School, began to come within the range of Soviet industry as a result of the progress of industrialisation under the terms of the First Five Year Plan

(1928-1933). For the naval defence of the USSR the Young School stressed the value of mines, submarines, aircraft, torpedo boats and fast destroyers, along with coastal fortifications. These could be constructed by the USSR, and such construction was politically and ideologically acceptable. This was so because such forces would at least in part fulfil the immediate objective of securing a means of protecting the Soviet Union from a repeat of intervention and gave the Soviets some small measure of sea power. Moreover, of course, given the concern for the land forces, the limited role of the Navy could be rationalised effectively and used to conceal the fact that the Soviets lacked the ability to do anything other than concentrate upon such forces at that time. In addition, amid the ideological upheavals of that time and the imposition of doctrinal purity throughout the Soviet Union as part of the developing Stalinist theme of 'Socialism in One Country', the strength of the Young School lay precisely in its tying the Navy directly into a supporting role for land and air forces, the fundamental unity of military and naval strategy within a single political and defence philosophy being one of the cardinal features of Leninism. Moreover, the notions of numbers and mass, the assessing of power on the basis of a head count rather than by individual size and qualitative criteria, made this line of thought palatable to communist ideology on the grounds that it was supposedly more 'democratic' and 'proletarian' than notions that embraced 'imperialist' doctrines. Historically, of course, Russia has always assessed strength and waged war on the basis of numbers, and politically there was absolutely nothing to be gained by trying to vie with the 'imperialists' at their own game. To try to build along Mahanite lines, as the Old School would have wished, would merely condemn the Soviets to a long and fruitless chase. Far more realistic was an attempt to dispense with 'capitalist' notions and to embark upon the search for a 'socialist' solution to the problems of naval defence.

Soviet naval resurgence began to get under way after 1932 - the year the Pacific Fleet was reconstituted - under the terms of the Second Five Year Plan (1933-1937). The Soviet Navy had been slowly growing in the previous five years, but the inauguration of a major construction programme under the Plan marked the point when the Soviet Navy began to emerge from the doldrums. It also seemed to mark the triumph of the Young School because the initial construction programme favoured concept of 'active defence' with the Navy subordinate to a supporting role for the Army because of the emphasis placed on building light coastal forces, particularly submarines. But if it was a triumph for the Young School, and the Old School was officially disgraced in 1932, then it was a dubious and short-lived one. Within a couple of years of the start of the

Plan there were clear and unmistakable signs of a trend back to Old School concepts with the building of heavy surface units. These signs became more pronounced by the end of the 'thirties.

This development is difficult to interpret. Put simply, large ships were built because the Soviets had acquired the ability to build more and bigger ships simultaneously, itself a reflection of the industrial achievements registered under the First and Second Plans. The laying down of the first batch of six *Kirov*-class heavy cruisers in 1934/1935 was an achievement that simply would have been beyond the USSR some five years before, and it was only made possible at this time by Italian technical assistance. Subsequently France and then the USA were approached for help, the latter being approached in November 1936 with a view to securing assistance in building modern fast battleships. Plans were put in hand to build carriers, but the complexities involved in the design of such ships and their aircraft forced the Soviets to put back their construction either to the end of the Third or the start of the Fourth Five Year Plan (i.e. about 1942/43), the aim being to secure four aircraft carriers by about 1948. These developments showed the extent to which the Soviets had moved away from rigid Young School doctrine, if, indeed, they had ever fully adhered to it *per se* in the first place. The fact that the *Kirovs* began to be laid down in 1934 would suggest that given a lead time of up to two years, authorisation of such ships may well have taken place before the start of the Second Five Year Plan.

Clearly there is a problem of interpreting this change, but it would seem evident that the trend in naval development back to the notion of the continued importance of heavy surface units, present in all the major navies after 1934, must have played some part in shaping Soviet plans. The lapsing of limitation treaties and the clear intention of the major naval powers to resume capital ship construction cannot but have had some effect on Soviet naval deliberations. Furthermore, it would appear that the desire to have major surface units to tie down an enemy and to possess such ships as an indication of power and interest played a part in the Soviet development of oceanic forces. The Spanish Civil War (1936-1939) brought home to the Soviets their weakness at sea. Despite their possession of the largest submarine force in the world at that time, Soviet ships carrying supplies to the Republicans were sunk and the Soviets were unable to maintain their interests in Spain. The Old School had been correct: the submarine and sea power were not synonymous. Obviously, the course of international developments could be said to have played into the hands of those who wanted oceanic forces. The rise of Hitler and the evident drift of Japan towards general war in eastern Asia, plus the general isolation and disregard of the USSR in Europe throughout the 'thirties, were obvious and sound reasons for the Soviets to look to the state of their high seas forces.

Yet there was an obvious inconsistency in Soviet naval development. If carriers were to be at sea by 1948 then there can be no doubt that the Soviets were aiming to secure a balanced force for oceanic purposes. But the fleet would be totally imbalanced until that time, and hence incapable of conducting operations on the high seas. It is evident that the Soviets were aspiring to a high-seas role. The reconstituting of the Northern Fleet in 1933, the development of Murmansk in the wastes of the Arctic on the only sea not under the immediate control of another power, the creation of the world's largest submarine arm and then the construction of first cruisers and then battleships - two in the Baltic and one in the Pacific had been laid down by 1940 - all point to the evolution of the Soviet Navy beyond a mere coastal defence force, more than just an appendage of the Army.

But precisely why this evolution occurred and how such forces were to operate are obvious questions of interpretation that become almost impossible to answer rationally. Just how and in what ways the Navy was to function at sea given the state of Soviet naval aviation is unclear, because without organic air cover from carriers ships would be vulnerable and probably ineffective. Stalin once made the remark that there was no need to provide battleships with heavy AA defences because it was not intended that they should operate off the Americas, but given the lack of carriers, plus the lack of even small light carriers as makeweights (simply for experience) and the fact that Soviet shore-based naval aircraft were deliberately built for very short ranges, it is very difficult to see how the heavy units were supposed to operate at all outside coastal waters - and no one can be reasonably expected to build 35,000-ton battleships to keep them in harbour.

Three possible explanations can be put forward for Soviet naval strategy at this time. Firstly, it could be argued that Soviet arrangements were designed to meet purely defensive requirements - which was the case - involving not passive defence but the construction of light forces around a few but very powerful surface units. The prime function of these units, in this instance, would be as a deterrent or a focus of defence in the event of aggression, and they would naturally be an instrument of force for use in dealings with small neighbours that shared a coastline on a common sea.

Secondly, it is possible to see developments in terms of their being evolutionary, a step-by-step process to the obtaining of oceanic sea power. In this picture the development of light coastal forces can be regarded as the essential first step in the acquisition of some measure of power in certain critically important sea areas. Initially one can assert that this evolution bears all the signs of a time-lag between tactical planning and building, and then one may suggest that the evolution has all the signs of not having been thought through in a logical and coherent manner. In this sense the Soviet Union would be portrayed in the same manner as Imperial Germany in 1914 in that she embarked upon construction programmes to meet political and strategic needs without having fully considered how a fleet would be used to fulfil its tasks. But if these views are correct, and placed alongside persistent Soviet industrial weakness throughout the 'thirties, then the decision to postpone carriers until 1942-43 and, it is believed, subsequently to scrap them altogether, begins to make sense. With Soviet capacity to build armour, gun turrets and barrels still limited, and with little technical knowledge of modern gunnery control arrangements and even less of the design and operation of carriers, the deferring/cancellation of carrier construction represents a sensible limitation of objectives to secure the best possible return for a modest investment, consistent with Soviet industrial power. Much of the blame for not pushing carrier development was subsequently attributed to Stalin, after he was dead, and there are signs of the dictator's habitual and clumsy intervention, but those same signs can also be used to suggest that despite driving his country to the edge of industrial exhaustion by his exorbitant demands, he remained a realist in aiming to achieve what was within reach at that time.

The third possible explanation, however, is the one that fixes attention on Stalin's personal interventions, and it is the explanation that attempts to account for developments in irrational terms. Stated simply, the whole of Soviet naval construction can be seen in terms of Stalin's personal prejudices and preferences taking priority over planned staff appreciations. Given our knowledge of Stalin's control over all aspects of Soviet society at this time and his adoption of targets, policies and acts hardly noted for their realism and moderation, any idea that the Soviet Navy somehow remained immune would hardly seem sensible. Granted the fact that Stalin more than decimated the officer corps of the Army and the Navy during the Purges, it is hard to believe that Stalin would ever have shown indulgence to their plans. Stalin loved heavy surface units. He actually physically liked to be on a big warship, and while it would be a gross exaggeration to assert that the *Kirov* became his retreat from the Kremlin, there is no doubt that the sense of power and grandeur, the trappings of office and (dare one say it) majesty, explicit in heavy ships, made a deep appeal to Stalin and perhaps in some way fulfilled some need on the part of this tyrant. This is not to say that the surface ships were built because Stalin wanted to treat them as his own

101

personal toys and have banquets on them as often as he could (and did), but it does point to Stalin developing the surface forces primarily as status symbols rather than practical weapons systems. This interpretation of events, however ludicrous it may seem, does have the virtue of explaining one (out-of-context) development. The post-war construction of the *Sverdlov*-class cruisers makes absolutely no sense in any rational strategic, tactical and technical context, but it does in personal terms. As Khrushchev remarked about the *Sverdlovs*, they were useful only in entertaining dignatories, and this may well have been what Soviet heavy ship construction in the inter-war period was about.

But whatever explanation of events is accepted, what is clear is that when war came to the USSR in June 1941 the Soviet Navy was caught in some form of transitional period. But by 1941, even if it had yet to grow into its strength, the Navy should have been able to have fought a reasonably successful defensive action, given its own size, the weakness of its enemies at sea and the fact that its forces always had to operate close to sources of support. In fact the Soviet Navy generally failed to wage effective rearguard actions with any degree of success, and it totally failed to undertake any form of tactical offensive that alone could have compensated for its strategic weaknesses and failures.

This was not entirely the Navy's fault. Much of the responsibility for this lay in Stalin's miscalculation in his ability to keep the USSR out of a general war in which he had no major land ally to tie down the strength of an enemy. This led to much of European Russia being overrun in the first weeks of war as a result of the lunatic deployment of Soviet forces forward in areas from which they could not withdraw. In the first weeks of war the Soviets incurred a series of colossal defeats, any one of which would have finished a western army. In the first five disastrous months of the Nazi-Soviet conflict the Soviets lost over 5,000,000 soldiers as prisoners alone as the Germans pushed the Soviet Army back to the outskirts of Leningrad and Moscow and to the banks of the Don.

Because of the large element of strategic and tactical surprise achieved by the Germans in June 1941 the Soviet Navy was condemned to labour under the immense handicap of enemy air supremacy in the period 1941-1943. These handicaps proved virtually insurmountable as the Navy assumed a tactically defensive role in support of ground forces, and its effectiveness failed to increase as the tide of war changed - largely because its early losses had gone too deep. Losses in ships and manpower had been very severe, and of the two the latter was probably the more serious. The Soviet Navy lost the cream of its manpower as they were sucked into the desperate land battles of 1941, and the Navy never really recovered from their loss. Subsequent replacements were simply under-trained, inexperienced and too short on morale to operate effectively. (It should always be remembered that even today 90 per cent of the Soviet people never see the sea in their lives.) The ships and equipment such non-maritime men fought, moreover, tended to be inadequate. Radar development, communications, hydrophones, sonar and anti-mine techniques were all aspects of naval technology and warfare where the Soviet Navy was years behind other naval combatants.

It was a scathing condemnation of the Soviet Navy that a force that went to war with a minimum strength in European waters of three battle-ships, nine cruisers, 75 destroyers, 157 submarines and various other minor units should consider one of its greatest successes of the war to be the sinking by submarine of the 25,484-ton passenger ship *Wilhelm Gustloff* with the loss of about 6,000 lives on the night of 30-31 January 1945. Even this achievement needs to be set against the simple fact that in conditions of overwhelming Soviet naval and air supremacy the Germans still managed to evacuate about 2,116,000 soldiers and civilians by sea from isolated pockets on the Baltic in the last five months of the war. This they did with an overall loss rate of 1 per cent. While the Soviets have, for propaganda purposes, made great play of the contribution of the Navy to the defence of Leningrad and the fact that more than a hundred amphibious operations were carried out in the course of the war, the fact remains that the Navy's impact on events was not even marginal. The official British naval history puts German losses to Soviet naval action as 214 merchantmen (445,526 tons) and 114 warships (63,255 tons), the overwhelming part of the losses coming in 1944 and 1945, not when the Soviet Navy needed to register success in 1941 and 1942.

At the end of the war the Soviet Navy could have been forgiven if it had a *déjà vu* attitude to the situation in which it found itself. The problem of its role, reconstruction and composition were much the same as they had been two decades earlier, and, of course, its development was certain to be restricted by the dominance of the Army in Soviet defence councils and the extent of devastation wrought by war. With some 20,000,000 Soviet citizens killed and the whole of western Russia shattered, the obvious Soviet priorities had to be simply to feed its population - no easy task given the ending of American aid - and industrial reconstruction. Anglo-American development of nuclear weapons immediately imposed upon the Soviet Union the need to acquire such weapons for herself, while her ground forces, which in taking Berlin spent itself and lost more men that the British armed forces lost in the entire war, needed a vast programme of re-equipment. It was inevitable that the Soviet Navy after 1945 should find itself, once more, at the bottom of the list of priorities with certain question marks placed against its future role.

The war brought formidable gains for the Soviet Union and a buffer zone in eastern and central Europe. Through her physical occupation of part of a divided Germany the USSR obtained a degree of security on land that had always eluded Russia. But in 1945 the only power with the means of opposing or threatening the USSR was, of course, the USA, infinitely more powerful than the Soviet Union and whose main strength was at sea and in the air, not that her land armies were by any means derisory. American power at sea was such that the position of the Soviet Navy in comparison was utterly hopeless. There was absolutely no point in even beginning to build a force with a view to challenging the Americans on the high seas. As we have seen, in 1945 the US Navy was the possessor of no less than 123 carriers of all types, launched or in service. The building of large numbers of surface units, even with carriers, on the part of the Soviets would do no more than provide the Americans with live target practice in the event of war. Stalin and the Navy were caught in an impossible situation. American naval power was envied for the flexibility it conferred on the USA and as the means by which the Americans could intervene almost anywhere in the defence of their interests. The Soviets dearly would have loved such a capability, but for the moment even a minor deterrence and defensive role was beyond the Soviets. At all costs the Soviets, in their normal process of taking precautions against a possible enemy, had to aim at building naval forces whose existence would either deter direct aggression or, in the event of failure, be able to defend Soviet coasts against attack. In the long term, after the 1950 authorisations when the worst of the ravages of war had been set right, the Soviet Union committed itself to build up a large navy with strong surface forces that included carriers as part of a balanced fleet. But in the short term the Soviets had no option but to revert to Young School notions, even though it was recognised that light coastal forces, submarines and land-based aircraft could not hope to prove effective against the mass and balance of the American (and British) fleets. The Soviet naval failure during the war and the American success in Atlantic and Pacific alike was more than enough proof of the validity of Old School ideas, but there was no choice in the matter. The state of the Soviet economy, the domination of the Army within a unified defence ministry (1947-1950) and the immediate need to have some presence in the four major sea areas around the Soviet Union ensured that there was no other course than to rationalise weakness and necessity and make the Navy the adjunct of the Army. Nevertheless, the Navy was not slow in recognising the obvious lesson of both the Pacific and Atlantic wars -

that naval warfare was about control of sea-borne lines of communication. Faced by potential opponents that were totally dependent on their vulnerable lines of communication by sea to survive and to maintain their forces in Europe, the moral to be drawn from German failure was obvious. Had the Germans begun the war with the strength that they had intended to have, the outcome of the war would have been very different. The implications for the Soviets was very clear.

But if the post-war period began with the Soviet Navy very much on the strategic (and inter-departmental) defensive, it was very active in two fields - the search for a tactically offensive role as compensation for strategic weakness and in research and development. The significance of these two elements was that their maturing in the course of the 'fifties lay at the base of the vast expansion of Soviet naval power in the 'sixties and 'seventies.

The search for a tactically offensive role was the natural outcome of the Soviets heeding their fleet's failings in a purely defensive role in the war. The means to carry out an offensive role were unstintingly promised, in 1945 the Soviets initiating a 20-year construction programme that scheduled the building of forty cruisers, 210 destroyers, 180 escorts and a staggering total of 1,200 submarines. Immediately the Soviets put in hand the completion of various ships, some of them on the stocks since 1939, simply to clear the slips for future construction, and authorised the *Zulu* and 336-strong *Whisky* classes of submarine, both apparently based on the design of surrendered German Type XXI U-boats. Subsequently, in 1947, the Soviets authorised the construction of 570 *Romeo*-class submarines and about 100 *Quebecs,* their construction to be put in hand once the *Whisky* and *Zulu* classes were well in hand. At the same time as the *Whiskys* began to take shape the Soviets projected the *Kotlin* and *Skoryi* classes of destroyers, seemingly based on contemporary western ships, and the heavy *Stalingrad* and light *Sverdlov* cruisers. In fact the production of these ships never really began to get under way until the period 1949/50, and none of the *Stalingrads* were completed. If rationalism is accepted as the basis of Soviet surface ship construction, it would appear that the cruisers at least were intended to fulfil a dual role, first as raiders to complement a submarine offensive on the high seas against western lines of communication and subsequently as major escorts in the event of a more balanced fleet evolving. The *Skoryis,* similarly, were more properly destroyer leaders rather than destroyers, and their authorisation may have been made with one eye on their possible use as command ships in flotillas operating with a fleet.

At that time (around 1947) two further developments were in train. Firstly, Soviet nuclear and missile research programmes must have been advanced far enough for the Soviets to authorise the conversion of the *Zulus* and the construction of the *Golf*-class submarines to carry surface-to-surface missiles. The programmes for these classes were set for the mid-'fifties, once other conventionally-armed submarines had been built and, presumably, when the development programmes of such weapons would have been finalised. Secondly, both the pace of construction and its direction seemingly altered significantly in 1949 or 1950. Four carriers were added to the long-term construction programmes. One can only speculate that this decision came about as a result of the hardening of suspicion between East and West into glacial hostility with the onset of the Cold War and the formation of the North Atlantic Alliance (1949). This decision to build carriers at some future date was probably related to the fact that by 1949/50 the US Navy had been reduced to a seven-carrier fleet. It may very well be that by about 1950 the Soviet Navy, in that year reconstituted as a separate ministry, glimpsed the possibility of emerging from the Americans' shadow. (If indeed this was the case, such hopes were disappointed. The Korean War (1950-1953) re-established the pre-eminence of the carrier within a US Navy which had been in something of a depression since the formation of the US Air Force and the securing of the strategic nuclear role by the Strategic Air Command. Eleven carriers saw action off Korea, and in 1953 the US Navy possessed an eighteen-carrier fleet. For many years US carrier strength never fell below sixteen.) Be that as it may, construction was certainly increased. After 1950 submarine construction which had averaged about twelve a year (mostly coastal boats) was stepped up to between sixty and eighty, and by 1958 the Soviets had an estimated 475 submarines of all types in service, despite cut-backs in the follow-on classes in 1954. While far short of the 1,200 planned for 1965, this was a total greater than the strength of the Kriegsmarine at any time during the Second World War.

By 1954-1957, however, this most ambitious of construction programmes was in confusion, the death of Stalin in March 1953 leading to a power-struggle for the succession within the Kremlin of which the Navy was an early casualty. In this struggle Khrushchev ultimately prevailed, and Khrushchev had little understanding of naval matters, was closely associated with the Army high command (to whom he owed his position and probably his life) and was primarily concerned with the Soviets acquiring strategic nuclear weapons, the Soviet Union's position of strategic inferiority to the USA being his over-riding concern. Ironically his attempts to redress the nuclear balance only resulted in its being tipped ever more against the Soviets in his period of power, but he did establish the basis by which the USSR acquired nuclear parity in the 'seventies - and he made an indelible imprint on the Navy.

For the Navy the Khrushchev era was critical in two respects. Firstly, it survived the period. Secondly, it received in 1955 a new commander, Gorshkov. The two were inter-related, so much so that now in 1981, a quarter of a century after his appointment, Gorshkov still remains in command and presides over a fleet he saved from emasculation by Khrushchev and watched grow under both Khrushchev and his successors.

The early years of the Khrushchev era were very difficult ones for the Navy because Khrushchev saw the Navy solely in terms of local defence and in 1954 was instrumental in abandoning the large fleet concepts of Stalin's day. Missilery played into his hands because the development of such weapons as the SS-N-2 *Styx* and the OTH-range *Strela/Scrubber* SS-N-1 and *Shaddock* SS-N-3 offered the Soviets ways of short-circuiting western superiority in gunnery and naval aircraft. Such missiles, especially the *Styx* which could be carried in very small coastal craft, packed a very substantial punch out of all proportion to the carrier's size and sea-going capabilities. The most dramatic demonstration of this came in 1967 when the Israeli destroyer *Eliat* was sunk by *Styx* missiles from a Soviet-supplied Egyptian fast patrol boat that did not leave harbour to engage. With three hits out of four (the last missed because the *Eliat* went down too quickly for her to be hit a fourth time), the *Styx* demonstrated the hopeless vulnerability of conventionally armed large surface units, particularly when surprised, to even the least prepossessing of inshore craft. It showed, moreover, the limitations that could be imposed on the exercise of sea power by even the most powerful of oceanic forces by the presence of such weapons in the hands of the least developed Third World country with a coastline and access to such technology.

Missiles such as the *Styx* therefore gave the Soviet Union some degree of security against amphibious assault, no force daring to approach a coastline until such weapons were neutralised. This lessened the immediate need for a large number of conventionally-armed surface units to pose a deterrence and offer defence against sea-borne invasion, and undoubtedly the development of SSMs played an important part in the construction cuts of 1954 and 1957. But Khrushchev would have gone much further. For Khrushchev there was no question of fighting, surviving and winning a strategic nuclear exchange, and hence the creation of large balanced fleets to fight for command of the seas - a concept of material use to its possessors only in the event of his having the time to exploit its advantages for a given purpose - was meaningless. To Khrushchev strategic nuclear weapons made large conventional ground and naval forces obsolete. But *Strela* and *Shaddock,* and then *Sark*

(SS-N-4) and *Serb* (SS-N-5), offered two distinct possibilities. These missiles offered the theoretical possibility of taking on American carriers, in Soviet eyes *the* naval threat to the Soviet Union, while the latter two missiles, being ballistic nuclear weapons, again offered the theoretical possibility of being able to strike at American cities. This was only theoretical. The *Strela,* with a reputed range of 150 nautical miles and the *Shaddock* (350 nautical miles) lacked any terminal guidance while the *Sark* (300 nautical miles) and *Serb* (750 nautical miles) had to be carried initially in conventional diesel-powered submarines, and none of these missiles could be fired from a submerged platform. Without any means of in-flight control missile-carrying submarines could not hope to engage American carriers that were not beyond the horizon, and any Soviet submarine commander willing to come to the surface to loose off his weapons in such circumstances would certainly have needed to have paid up his life insurance premiums. Similarly the notion of Soviet submarines breaking into the North Atlantic to lie undisturbed and on the surface off American cities was equally unrealistic. The 1962 Cuban Missile Crisis showed that the US Navy had full measure of all Soviet submarines in the North Atlantic and there was certainly no possibility *at that time* of Soviet submarines posing a genuine strategic threat to mainland USA.

But, and here was the important proviso, however limited the capacity of such missiles and submarines as the *Zulu V* class were to carry out both a strategic and a tactical role, they remained the first stage of a process that had to lead to the creation of an invulnerable sea-borne nuclear deterrent within a relatively short time. The cuts-back in conventional construction in 1957 were vital in this respect because they went hand in hand with the decision to begin incorporation of nuclear propulsion into future Soviet submarines (though the conventionally-powered *Foxtrot*-class of patrol submarines in fact were ordered simultaneously). Under the terms of the 1957-1958 decisions the *Whisky Longbins* were cut back, the *Golf*-class was taken in hand for conversion and the *Yankee*-class was authorised. To go alongside these strategic submarines, the *Juliet*-class was curtailed and modified and the *Echo*-class was projected. Both these classes carried medium range missiles for operations against surface units. At the same time the *November* and *Victor* classes of SSNs were authorised.

The fusion of missiles and nuclear propulsion for submarines therefore constituted a defensive move designed to secure and protect a workable deterrent and a means of trying to combat American naval strategic delivery systems, carriers and submarines alike. But the 1957-1958 decisions also saw a significant shift in the future development of surface units. Despite Khrushchev's sniping, Gorshkov was able to persuade the political leadership of the continued importance of surface units. The grounds on which Gorshkov managed this feat - which is a comment in itself on the consistency of Soviet policy and Khrushchev's rule - are not exactly clear, but it would seem that three main influences were at work. Firstly, Gorshkov argued along the lines of the Khrushchev thesis that surface units had lost their importance but added the more sublte shade of emphasis that stressed that they were not as important as they had been. From this it was possible to argue, as Gorshkov did, that this was certainly true about conventionally armed ships, but was not necessarily correct with respect to missile-armed ships and in terms of ASW. With the Americans beginning to develop their own medium range strategic weapons for submarines - such as the *Regulus* - ASW and sea power in general became increasingly important for the Soviets: and there still remained the NATO carriers. Secondly, sea power was becoming far more relevant to the Soviets because of the quickening pace of decolonialisation. Just as it had made no sense to aspire to an oceanic capability in the face of overwhelming American superiority, it had made no sense to seek any form of overseas presence at a time when the grip of the imperial powers was strong. But by the middle and late 'fifties, after the French defeat in Indo-China, with numerous campaigns being fought in various colonies and after the Anglo-French humiliation over Suez in 1956, it made far more sense to aspire to a serious oceanic capability as part of the Soviet aid to revolutionaries in their struggles for national liberation. Thirdly, there was a strong naval lobby. The strength of this lobby, and that of the corresponding military one, was to be seen during the arguments over the proposed 1960 cuts on defence spending. These cuts Khrushchev was forced to abandon, in large measure because of the open discontent they stirred up amongst the officer corps. But within the Navy the emphasis on missiles, submarines and coastal craft was not reflected by an overall balance of expenditure because of the various factions and pressure groups competing for funds for their particular specialisation or function. In any case a new generation of surface ships soon began to emerge. The *Sverdlovs, Kildins* and *Kyndas* were all cut back for modification with new versions, heavily armed with a mix of guns and missiles, taking their place on the stocks. The modified *Kyndas* that began to appear in 1962 probably represented the first purpose-built guided-missile warships in the world. Moreover, from these years date a new class, the *Moskva* class of A/S cruisers. These were built on abandoned *Stalingrad* hulls, but the initial programme of eight was reduced to two in 1961. The *Moskva* and *Leningrad* reflected an obvious concern to get into the ASW business, but they also reflected Soviet limitations in certain aspects of construction. One of their major weaknesses was that they drew 4-ft more at the bow than they did at the stern.

The 1957-1958 decisions were probably the most crucial of all those involving the Navy in the entire post-war period because they represented a deliberate movement away from any attempt to merely rival western sea power to harnessing new technology as a means of countering traditional western superiority at sea. In missilery the Soviets started more or less on equal terms with the West, and the programmes of these years showed that the Soviet Navy was no longer an imitative one. These decisions began to show results in the middle and late 'sixties, and one of the most misunderstood features of the Cuban Crisis was that it did not in fact alert the Soviets to the importance of sea power and balanced surface forces. The massive expansion of the Soviet Navy in the late 'sixties and 'seventies was not the outcome of Cuba: the expansion had been foreshadowed by decisions that pre-dated that débâcle for Soviet status and diplomacy.

In the last decade Soviet construction and the size of the Soviet Navy have become increasingly difficult to interpret. By 1970 Soviet naval strength had begun to seriously concern the West for the first time, and this was only two or three years after British Defence Secretary Healey's famous remark to the effect that in the event of war Soviet naval forces in the Mediterranean had a life expectancy of minutes. There was no doubting that he was correct, though in those minutes Soviet ships might well have achieved their purpose; in Soviet eyes ships are expendable once they have served their offensive purpose. But in general terms the Americans could have eliminated these forces and pushed their carriers into the Greenland-Iceland-UK gap. Any Soviet attempt to use air and surface units against the Americans would have been dealt with by carrier Phantoms, and American SSNs were more than a match for noisy and vulnerable *Zulu V, Juliet* and *Echo* submarines. But in the 'seventies, in the appropriate and telling phrase of Michael MccGwire, the Soviet Navy changed from being something for which there was 'a need to have to nice to have'. By the end of the 'seventies the 'nice to have' had begun to assume ever more ominous dimensions since it became evident that Soviet capacity at sea was far larger than any immediate defensive need and there were no signs of any abatement in the tempo of construction.

If anything, the pace and diversity of Soviet construction in the 'seventies quickened with the building of new types of ships that reflected the widening horizons and ambitions of the Soviet Navy. The two most spectacular and significant developments were the public debuts of the *Kiev* in 1975 and the *Kirov* in 1980, both exceptionally graceful ships.

The *Kiev,* the lead ship of a class of four and subsequently joined in service by the *Minsk,* is a 43,000-ton CVS with a 600-ft angled flight deck. Her air group is about 35-strong with about twelve VTOL Yak-36 Forgers, twenty A/S Hormone A helicopters and three guidance-relay Hormone Bs. In addition to her group she carries an armament the like of which simply does not appear on any western carrier. She has both SA-N-3 and SA-N-4 missiles, 30-mm Gatlings and 76-mm guns, 250 n.m. ranged SS-N-12 missiles, a twin SUW-N-1 launcher and two MBU 2500A firers, the latter two being A/S weapons systems. She also has the capacity to lift about a battalion of naval infantry. In short, she is an extremely powerful ship. She is strongly equipped defensively and offensively with missiles, has an amphibious capability and in part fulfils the need for some form of air capability for the fleet at sea. The *Kirov,* seemingly, will also aid the cause of Soviet air defence at sea. She is the first of a class of possibly two but more probably four 27,000-ton cruisers which are nuclear-powered. The *Kirov* carries twelve SA-N-6 and two SA-N-4 launchers, and twenty SS-NX-19 launchers. Like the *Kiev,* the *Kirov* carries SS-N-14 missiles and (presumably) Hormone B helicopters as well as an organic A/S capability in addition to her Hormone As.

With such a formidable array of defensive firepower it seems difficult to believe that the two/four *Kirovs* can be anything other than escorts for the *Kievs,* or proper carriers, as and when they enter service. Since a number of *Kirovs* are to be built with nuclear propulsion, it is inconceivable that they should be employed in the Baltic and Black Seas; it must be the Soviet intention to divide them between the Northern and Pacific Fleets, and this must involve an offensive oceanic role. It is perhaps not without significance that the *Minsk* seems to be permanently based in Camranh Bay, Vietnam, and it may well be that she with a *Kirov* or two might be held in that area for political and photogenic reasons. The general area is a vital one, its significance being often forgotten by western Europe. Camranh Bay, as the Japanese Navy showed in 1941, is well within striking range of the Malay Barrier and The Philippines and lies across Japanese lines of communication with south east Asia and beyond. A Soviet naval force in the Bay is a useful support to Vietnam in her dealings with China and a counter to the American VIIth Fleet. The political mileage to be gained from the presence of such good looking ships in an American-built base and in an area which has been the VIIth Fleet's backyard since 1945 is likely to be considerable. The whole of south east Asia, with its immense natural wealth, is a volatile area, and the deployment of a Soviet task force in Vietnamese waters is hardly likely to lessen tensions there. In any event the political impact of a *Kirov* when one makes its way east is certain to be substantial as she shows the flag at Dakar, Luanda, Maputo and in India.

Balanced surface forces will obviously come one step nearer when the first of the carriers enters service, and this cannot be delayed for much longer. Inevitably the first carrier, being built at Severodvinsk, must be a medium carrier, approximately 55,000 tons or slightly larger than the recently retired *Ark Royal*. It seems very unlikely that she will operate VTOL aircraft because she has catapaults and arrester gear, and it could be that she will operate up to sixty aircraft, possibly Mig-27 Flogger Ds. On past performance it would be surprising if within ten years of entering service she was not followed by an attack carrier of *Nimitz*-proportions. There seems no good reason to believe that the Soviets will accept permanent inferiority to the Americans in this the last remaining area of clear western superiority in naval warfare.

The construction of large surface units that are certain to increase Soviet intervention ability and oceanic capabilities throughout the world must be seen in conjunction with naval building in other directions. The deployment to the Pacific, after service in the Mediterranean, of the *Ivan Rogov*, an 11,000-ton LPD, inevitably foreshadows the future delivery of more such large and sophisticated amphibious warfare ships. She would seem to indicate not simply a major qualitative advance over earlier assault ships but a possible Soviet interest in at least securing the means by which they could pursue forward policies in east and south east Asia. The emergence of a purpose-built hospital ship from Gdansk in Poland for the Soviet Navy (built at a time when Britain was subsidising the building of Polish merchantmen in UK yards) may not seem to amount to very much in itself, but such a ship does assume some significance when the obvious questions of her need and purpose are asked. At the very least the building of such a specialised and expensive auxiliary illustrates the seriousness with which the quest for sea power is regarded by the Soviets: at worse it would seem to indicate a willingness to develop all the auxiliaries (including such ships as the *Berezina* and her three successors) needed to support an interventionist capability.

Such developments evidently lie close to the heart of Gorshkov, but so too does the continued expansion and modernisation of the Soviet merchant marine, publicly stated by him to be the indispensable supporting arm in the overall Soviet capability for overseas ventures. By equally open admission, the development of the merchant marine has been prompted by both commercial and non-commercial strategic reasons, a facet that once more points to the basic integration of political, military and economic policies in Soviet thinking.

Certainly, there are good economic reasons for the Soviets developing their marine. It still remains easier, quicker and cheaper to move certain commodities between European Russia and the Maritime Provinces by sea rather than by rail. (This is likely to change. The expansion of the carrying capacity of the Trans-Siberian Railway, the administration of which significantly comes under the Foreign Trade Ministry, may reverse this situation and could well attract some of the trade between western Europe and the Far East away from the sea.) The merchant navy, like that of Britain, is a major currency earner. In fact it is the fourth largest earner of foreign currency after oil, timber and diamonds, and its earnings by the beginning of the 'seventies - that is until the failure of the Soviet grain harvests became habit - was beginning to cover Soviet deficits on visible trade with the West. For a country with an accumulated debt to the West of at least $18,000 million, a deficit on current trade that cannot be rectified by any significant increase in its exports and with very few finished goods that it can sell on world markets, the earnings of the merchant service are vital.* Equally, the activities of the Soviet fishing fleet are critically important to a country whose agricultural sector is notoriously inefficient.

These aspects of Soviet mercantile development pose no concern to the West, and it is only to be expected that the USSR, in a manner befitting so powerful a state, should seek to possess a large and efficient marine in the same way that many states have built up national air lines for reasons of prestige. Yet western shipping lines have become increasingly concerned over the last decade about Soviet trading policies and the activities of the Soviet merchant navy. It can meet Soviet strategic and economic needs, but, from all the evidence, it is still being expanded and modernised at a considerable rate, or at least a rate that could be considered unjustifiably high in terms of the Soviet Union's own national commercial requirements. Western anxieties have risen because of five inter-related considerations. Firstly, the Soviet marine has expanded at a far greater rate than the growth in world trade in general and Soviet trade in particular, and this excess capacity can only earn money if used on routes in which the Soviets have no direct national interest. There is no room for new ships to be used on existing Soviet lines. Secondly, the Soviets in the 'seventies began to concentrate newer shipping in cross trade (i.e. trade between two other nations) and undercut western lines in some cases by up to 50 per cent, presumably as the means of establishing a share in the market. Thirdly, the Soviets have consistently refused to reconsider their pricing policies. Their merchantmen do not carry insurance, do not have to cover depreciation costs and have access to subsidised fuel. At various international shipping conventions they have

* Soviet merchant fleet earnings in 1977 have been estimated at $1,000m. The capital cost is not available but must increase with a relatively ageing fleet.

refused to consider limitation of their market share or have demanded a share out of all proportion to past or present interest. Fourthly, the Soviets, by the manipulation of c.i.f. sale and f.o.b. purchase terms of trade, have insisted upon a heavily protectionist policy towards its own trade with western states. At the present time at least 75 per cent of all British, Japanese and West German trade with the USSR by sea is carried in Soviet bottoms because the Soviets can pick off western firms by insisting on their carrying the goods as a price for giving the contract. The West has proved incapable of formulating any response to this situation. American anti-trust legislation has frustrated any attempt to secure American participation in response to Soviet practices, while within the EEC no concerted action has been possible because of French hostility to any proposal that would counter Soviet interests. Fifthly, and here, possibly, is the main fear, in the next five years Soviet cellular and ro/ro vessels are expected to increase by at least 65 per cent - representing a 120 per cent increase between 1975 and 1985 - and this can only mean ever greater pressure on western shipping lines, particularly those engaged in traditional cross trade in Third World Areas. Even allowing for an inevitable shrinking of market share as recently independent states begin to develop their own marines, western lines fear long-term bankruptcy since they cannot compete with heavily subsidised state lines that seem intent on using non-commercial practices in an aggressively mercantilist manner to disrupt established shipping patterns. The very real fear expressed in some circles is that in the course of time the Soviets could come to dominate Third World trade with the result that the West, which relies on the Third World for its raw materials, energy, food and markets, could become vulnerable to Soviet economic pressure in waters outside the NATO sea area. The long term danger is that if lines are forced into liquidation the West could become dependent on the Soviets for the carrying of essential strategic raw materials with a corresponding loss of freedom of decision at some future date. Whereas the USSR is more or less self-sufficient in the thirteen key strategic raw materials, the West is dependent on imports from the Third World in nine cases to meet more than 90 per cent of its needs.

Thus the vast expansion of Soviet military and economic power at sea over the last two decades has caused uneasiness in certain western circles, and has given rise to considerable political and professional debate over Soviet intentions. The obvious questions of whether these developments constitute a threat and, if so its extent, are obvious political issues, dependent in part on personal and political perspective. They are questions that are difficult to answer, but any attempt to even begin to answer them must place Soviet naval and mercantile developments in a dual context. Firstly, sea power is the only area of military activity where the West still retains any degree of superiority over the Warsaw Pact. In every other area, in the air, on land and with respect to strategic missiles, the West is in a position of numerical inferiority, and its traditional qualitative superiority has been and still is being eroded. At sea the same process is being repeated whereby the West is firmly established on a declining scale of strength and effectiveness. Having come so close to superiority at sea already, it seems hardly likely that the Soviets will call a halt to their efforts. Secondly, at the 25th Congress of the CPSU (1976) Foreign Minister Gromyko stated that the purpose of Soviet strengthening of their forces is to deny options to the West at some crisis in the future.

Of course Gromyko has been proved wrong in his assertions of Soviet intentions in the past, Czechoslovakia in 1968 and Afghanistan in 1979 being two obvious instances where there was something of a credibility gap between what he said were Soviet intentions and what actually happened, and the degree of reliance that can be placed on such an observation is a matter of personal choice. But it is a comment that sets the continued expansion of Soviet sea power in its proper place. It is not an isolated phenomenon, and it must be seen as one part of a major effort over the last twenty years to strengthen every aspect of the Soviet war machine. It is evident that Soviet strength is far in excess of any immediate defensive need, short of full-scale nuclear exchange. It is also evident that even allowing for Soviet concern for eastern Europe's passivity and safety and the security of their very costly merchant fleet, the continued expansion of the Backfire bomber force and the completion of SSNs at a rate of one a month can hardly be portrayed as defensive arrangements, even in defending Warsaw against the Poles.

What is evident about the Soviet naval build-up is that it has long since met the initial defensive requirement to deny western navies access to waters that wash the Soviet Union. In Gorshkov's own writings in a series of articles in *Morskoi Sbornik* in 1972-1973 reference was made not to securing command of the seas in the manner that Britain and the USA commanded the seas in their respective eras of naval supremacy, but to securing 'command of the sea in the theatre of war or in part of that theatre'. This can only mean that in war the Soviet Navy must aim to secure command, or at the very least deny an enemy command, of waters in which it has a direct operational interest. By any rational standard the combination of ocean-going and coastal warships available to the Soviets more than ensures that the Soviets have projected their strategic frontiers forward over hundreds of miles at sea in order to provide defence in depth for Mother Russia. By following on Gorshkov's notion of denying

115

an enemy access to waters 'in the theatre of war', it could be expected that the primary task of surface units of the Northern Fleet in the event of war would be to extend the area of denial to the Arctic where the Soviets will undoubtedly concentrate their latest and best SSBMs, the 32-strong *Delta* class. Even though Gorshkov has taken pains to stress that the offensive is a form of warfare superior to the defence at sea, it would appear unlikely that Soviet surface units would attempt amphibious operations in northern Norway (overland and airborne operations would seem quicker, easier and safer) or to carry out thrusts into the North Sea or to operate as raiders or a battle force in mid-Atlantic. These options seem improbable because the Soviets are unlikely to believe that at the present time they have sufficient force for an attack to be decisive, and they would be wary of pushing their surface forces too far forward. This would not be for fear of loss. The sinking of NATO warships or forcing their return to port to re-arm is justification for their own losses because the sea is not so important to Soviet survival as it is to NATO countries. The Soviet bloc is in most respects self-sufficient for the waging of offensive operations because it can draw from its resources in Eurasia, but the NATO countries have no such facility. The disruption of NATO lines of communication across the Atlantic would be a task for long-range bombers and the conventional and nuclear-powered sub-marines, and NATO would have the task of ensuring sea denial into the North Atlantic for these boats. Given the strength of the submarine arm -200 Soviet conventional submarines and 87 nuclear submarines of all types other than SSBMs - it is hard to see how the Americans would dare risk moving their carriers eastwards unless and until western SSNs had fought for and secured an overwhelming victory in the Atlantic. In the event of a general war American carriers would be extremely vulnerable, and their safest location would probably be the Caribbean. In any event it is likely that the Soviet Navy will achieve the denial of the use of certain waters to NATO forces even before the start of a war and even achieve the denial of the use of the high seas for what could prove to be a decisive period of a war - if it was short and conventional.

There exists, therefore, the probability that the Soviet Navy has already or shortly will reduce the US Navy to a mid-Atlantic or even a western-Atlantic force. Perhaps this represents the most important shift in the naval balance of power since 1945 because it is certain to affect the ability of the USA to support her European allies in time of war. This is an achievement that could hardly be registered by a fleet built for defensive purposes; the sheer scale of Soviet investment in its Navy can hardly be justified in defensive terms. It is clear that the Soviets regard their Navy in an offensive light in the sense that without it they could not hope to influence events outside their own immediate land area. Throughout Gorshkov's writings there is an almost Darwinian strain - one is tempted to say a line of thought that would recommend itself to Nietzche, Kjellén and Hitler - that lays emphasis on the notion that rich and powerful states in history have been those with powerful navies and that those states that have neglected their sea power are those that have had their day. Clearly Gorshkov regards the Navy as a sign of Soviet determination to survive, and equally clearly the Soviets see their Navy as an instrument of policy, being able to threaten war, being able to conduct limited operations well below the threshold of general war, being a 'negotiating chip' in diplomatic exchanges and in general adding to the dignity, status and strength of the Soviet Union. Gorshkov lays great stress upon the 'showing the flag' role as a means of winning friends, influencing and impressing people and in general establishing a presence in areas where Soviet presence could not otherwise manifest itself. It is clear from Gorshkov's writings that he regards the Navy as the means of ensuring that the division of the seas into EEZs is not a process that can be carried out without the USSR having a very large say in deliberations. In this respect, and in conjunction with the use of the navy as an instrument of force for a political aim, Soviet actions in the dispute with Norway over the division of the Barents Sea and the future status of Svalbard are illuminating. Though no final agreement has been worked out, the Soviets have offered Norway a bilateral deal over Svalbard and accepted an interim arrangement over the Barents Sea with one part of it divided between them. Despite the existence of Norwegian quota arrangements with Britain and West Germany to fish in these shared waters, Soviet naval ships have harassed British and German trawlers to the point where they have all but abandoned the area - but the Norwegians have been left alone. There is no doubt that in this one area of activity the Soviets have played a subtle game of offering blandishments, inducements and covert warnings to undermine Norwegian concepts of deterrence and assurance in favour of appeasement.

Sea power, moreover, is to the Soviets the means of underpinning client states and ensuring that the final say in overseas ventures by proxy troops remains with the Soviet Union. Given Soviet adventurism in the 'seventies - Angola, Mozambique, the Horn of Africa, Eritrea, Kampuchea, Laos and Afghanistan - it is difficult to believe that the Soviets will show greater restraint in the 'eighties than they did in the 'seventies when they were weaker. If such comments appear neanderthal in that they represent a reactionary and orthodox 'Cold War' mentality, then it is reasonable to point out that given the closed nature of Soviet society and decision-making processes, the only possible criteria by which future intention may be assessed are political ideology, present capabilities and past performance, none of which can give any cause for re-assurance. It is as well to remember as the days to the appearance of the first Soviet carrier are counted down that since Zhukov's famous comments of 1957, the official Soviet line in political and naval publications has decried carriers as weapons fit only for aggressive imperialists and not peace-loving socialist states intent only on self defence. The rationalisations that will surround the appearance of the first Soviet carrier will make very interesting reading.

These comments, however, imply a rational explanation of developments, and almost unthinkable though the alternative may be, this could be the case. There is evidence to suggest that the Soviets really do not know what they are about at sea and that Soviet construction has staggered from one mistake to another. It could be argued that though the Soviets have the undoubted ability to build good ships and arm them well, there is no system in their construction and that they really have no clear idea of how to build and use a fleet. This is a view that would suggest that Soviet construction is less the result of any clear view but rather a response to various conflicting influences within the Soviet naval and political hierarchies, and it would further suggest that the Soviets have repeated (on a much larger scale) the mistakes of the inter-war period and, like the pre-1914 Imperial German Navy, have not really thought out the meaning of sea power and its strategic, tactical and technical aspects.

Certain aspects of Soviet naval development would confirm a lack of systematic appreciation of the purposes of sea power. The development of missilery in surface ships and submarines came at the very time when carriers ceased to be the major naval threat to the USSR and the massive concentration of Soviet resources on ASW in the early 'sixties coincided with the opening of SLBM ranges far beyond the effective endurance of current Soviet warships. At two quite separate times and in two quite different directions it is possible to argue that Soviet construction was entirely misdirected strategically, and even the concentration on the building of coastal craft in the post-war period could be regarded as hopelessly inopportune and irrelevant because there was never any real prospect of Anglo-American forces carrying out the types of operation against which the Soviets were making their preparations.

Moreover, there are certainly grave inconsistencies in ship and weapon development. SSM ranges began in the 350/750 n.m. bracket and subsequently came down to horizon range and less, but they have begun to rise again, almost as if the Soviets somehow believe that an inter-locking ranging pattern will in itself achieve results. Either the

Soviets are correct and have made a profound breakthrough in guidance and control that has so far eluded the west, or they do not know what they are doing. It is rather hard to believe that the Hormone B represents the qualitative technological advance required to solve the problems of in-flight correction for SSMs. The building of the *Kievs,* the *Kirovs* and the completion of the *Petropavlovsk* and *Tashkent* (end-runs of the *Kara*-class heavy ASW cruisers) seem totally irrational for a Navy that has consistently belittled the value of such large and vulnerable ships in the past — albeit at a time when they did not have any. Cruiser construction itself seems more than a little confused. The building of two (and perhaps even three) new classes of heavy ASW cruisers when the *Kara* and the *Kresta I* and *Kresta II* classes are already in existence seems insupportable. It must be admitted that the *Kresta II* cruisers are not used as escorts for the *Kievs* - in itself a little strange because it might be thought that such ships, like the ill-fated British *Bristol*-class, would have been well-suited to escort duties - and it may be that the new cruisers might therefore fulfil a perceived tactical need. If so, the development of both an 8,000-ton cruiser (already under trials with the designation Bal-Com 2) as a replacement for the *Kotlin* and *Kildin* classes and a 12,000-ton cruiser as a replacement for the *Kashins* seems incredible. To have perhaps as many as six or seven different classes of medium and heavy ASW cruisers in service at any given time hardly suggests a clear and settled order of priorities. While on the matter of oceanic forces it is as well to note that the 34,000-ton *Berezina* does not operate as a fleet auxiliary, and just why the Soviet Navy should built such a large and expensive auxiliary that would appear to have been purpose built to support *Kievs* and then not use her in such a role seems at the very least surprising.

Nor can the matter of ship armament be ignored since the arming of Soviet ships seems more geared to the filling of otherwise empty space -at what price to damage control arrangements? - than to serve tactical need. The *Kiev* is equipped with ASW torpedo tubes, and both she and the *Kirov* carry MBU 2500A A/S mortars. There would seem no logical reason why such heavy units should be equipped with (short range) depth charges and even with A/S missiles. That they are so equipped seems to reflect the Soviet obsession with keeping tried and proved weapons systems in service, irrespective of need and tactical function. Both ships have ageing and mid-performance radars, and this is an area where one would have reasonably expected the Soviets to have developed new and more sophisticated equipment. There are so many strange features about some of the Soviet ships that one is left with the unanswerable question of what it is that the Soviets think that they can do with them. The *Kirov* would seen an obvious case in point. As a 32,000-ton battle cruiser she seems somewhat large for a carrier escort. She has nuclear propulsion, which could either be an abberation or a sign of a whole new development in Soviet ships. For all her defensive firepower her very size, plus the fact that in the final analysis her real power is limited, must have resulted in her pendant number being noted with quiet satisfaction and a grim gallows humour by American carrier pilots. The building of a 600-ft 32,000-ton *Typhoon*-class submarine, nearly double the size of the latest American *Trident*-class seems fantastical. Her very size must be in some ways a limit on her operational effectiveness, and just why so large a submarine, and for what purpose, is baffling. It has been reported that she is to be equipped with sixteen SLBMs, and if true that would mean that despite her size she has much less offensive power than a *Trident*. She was on the stocks for the best part of a decade and was evidently beset with all kinds of construction and development problems, while her presumed armament, the new NE-04, has similarly encountered difficulties since the first test flight in January 1980.

Of course, overshadowing all these technical matters is the obvious question of how the Soviets can afford the manpower and money for this continuous construction and seemingly endless expansion of power. In Soviet eyes power is its own justification and the expansion of state power is an end in itself. The USSR has only achieved its present status, at least the equal of the USA, through immense effort, and the urge to sea power is but part of the quest to be strong (and hence secure) and to attain recognition and status. The impetus towards sea power has obviously been part of an effort to make the Americans treat the Soviets on the basis of equality, which the Americans never did for two decades after the war, and this has clearly been the justification for what must have been a hideously expensive effort. But this really does not answer the questions of either how or why the Soviets can afford this effort. Undoubtedly western credits over the last two decades have enabled the Soviets to fund their armaments expenditure more easily than would otherwise have been the case, but even this does not really begin to explain how the Soviets can afford to take so much manpower, money and materials for the Navy out of an economy hardly renowned for its dynamic qualities. Even allowing for the fact that the ruling élite of the USSR has an utter disregard for the ordinary man in the street and has made no real attempt to develop a consumer economy, arms development must have warped the balance of Soviet industrial development and must be driving the Soviet Union towards bankruptcy. The Soviet economy is noted for its poor investment levels, low profitability and productivity and lack of sophistication, yet the demands that have been placed upon it in recent years have risen, not slackened. It is very difficult to resist the notion that given the fact that the arms industry is one of the very few efficient sectors of the economy, naval development over the last decade may well be in large part the result of the power of the military-industrial complex (of the kind Eisenhower warned his countrymen in respect to the USA in 1961) within the Soviet political hierarchy. There must be more than merely a hint of the suspicion that Soviet expansion across the whole range of naval activity is a reflection of the various internal divisions within the Navy. Indeed, perhaps the development of the Navy as a whole is a Frankenstein monster that has assumed a momentum of its own with the Soviets producing ships because they are good at producing ships because it is important to produce ships because there is need for a fleet which has to be equipped with ships.

Well-nigh crippling costs in money and manpower affect not just the Soviets, of course; they have been at the root of the relative decline of the Royal Navy over the last two decades. This decline, being so spectacular in terms of the loss of ships, has concealed the fact that until the last couple of years the Royal Navy remained without dispute the third largest oceanic force in the world. Its position has probably been taken over by the French by virtue of their continued possession of two CVVs. The British still retain a commando and an ASW carrier, and both could play a very limited CVV role, but the French possession of the *Foch* and *Clemenceau,* along with the light helicopter carrier *Jeanne d'Arc,* is probably enough to ensure a status second only to the super-powers at sea. If, indeed, the French press ahead with the construction of two nuclear-powered carriers as has been suggested then this will certainly confirm them in such a status, but it may well prove to be a dubious one. Though the French in the 'seventies began a programme of seventeen Type A69 frigates, of which eight were in service by mid-1979, their escort forces will remain small. Most of the destroyers and frigates in service with the French Navy date from the 'fifties, and the present building programmes will not cover natural wastage.

The French, however, have been concerned to build up their naval power as part of a deliberate attempt to secure a measure of sea power as the means of demonstrating French independence of and non-reliance upon the Americans and the North Atlantic Alliance. By dint of her geographical position France enjoys the benefits of NATO membership without having to undertake any obligations, and she has developed her Navy since the time of de Gaulle as one of the means by which she can pose as a great power and a nation that has to be taken into everyone's considerations. The main means by which this has been attempted is the 'force de dissuasion', the naval element of which consists of five SSBNs, a sixth having been ordered and laid down as the intermediate between the five *La Redoutables* and their replacements which are scheduled for the 'nineties. The French have also begun construction of SSNs, three having been ordered of which one, the *Provence,* has been launched. These, however, are much smaller than contemporary SSNs, and it would appear that these are very much weaker than normal hunter-killers.

Britain, just 44 per cent the size of France and a poorer country in terms of GNP, seemingly has been less able than France to adapt to change, and she has certainly encountered more problems in meeting the changing demands of sea power and to settle on a definite role for her fleet. In part this was occasioned by the ending of conscription under the terms of the 1957 Defence Review and continuing uncertainties about the availability of manpower. More profound, however, were the effects of relative industrial and financial decline of Britain throughout the post-war era which was coupled with a fundamental change of role, after the Suez débâcle, from an imperial sea power to a solely European state of second-class status (after West Germany and France) with just a few lingering outside commitments that were the legacies of an imperial past.

As late as 1960 the Royal Navy had a paper strength of 147 warships in service, with a further 42 units detailed for trials, weapons testing and training. A further 292 ships were in either reserve or various stages of refitting and modernisation, and these figures, which include a total of eight fleet carriers, 52 destroyers and 100 frigates, do not include a vast array of depot, maintenance and general service ships. Britain still remained second only to the USA in terms of oceanic naval power, and qualitatively the Royal Navy had a formidably high standard of professional expertise. She had pioneered angled flight decks, steam catapaults and landing mirrors for carriers in the post-war period, and even if the Suez operation showed many unsuspected weaknesses, the overall failure of the operation could not be put down to naval inadequacies. Even into the mid-'sixties Britain remained very powerful at sea, and British success in meeting the threat of Indonesian confrontation over the establishment of Malaysia (1963-1966) was largely the result of British naval power.

In many ways Malaysia was the swansong of the old Navy because it came to be caught between aspiration and inadequate performance on the part of the nation as a whole. As time passed the ramifications of the 1957 decisions became more evident because the Review committed Britain to high-cost armed services (because they were all volunteer and stood in need of weapons replacement the costs of which were rising) at a time when chronic entrenched economic problems ensured that there could be no increase in real spending on defence. Rather than deal with this problem at source by making a thorough re-evaluation of national role, resources and commitment, successive British governments have sought to make selective economies in all the services in the belief that the maintenance of a capability at sea, on land and in the air as well as strategic weapons, was both desirable and possible even for a nation no longer in the second rank.

As a result the story of the Royal Navy since 1957 has been one of constant uncertainty, and in part it had only itself to blame for this situation. If indeed the Indonesian Confrontation was the last success of British naval power, then its success was the result of a very curious and lopsided development of the Royal Navy in the post war period. The omnipotence of the US Navy in this period saw the Royal Navy drift away from a specifically fleet role - the Americans did not need any real help in that respect - into an amphibious capability that came to be tied up with what was called a 'peace-keeping role', mainly summed up by the phrase, 'East of Suez'. This was the natural legacy of an imperial past, and it was doomed on two counts. Firstly, the kind of force that the Royal Navy would be able to deploy in the late 'sixties east of Suez - a carrier with some forty aircraft and a brigade group - could only hope to be effective as long as there was no need to use it. The strength that Britain would be able to wield would be totally inadequate to take on real opposition, the experience of Aden (1963-1967) being proof of that, while the amphibious assault ships (seventeen in 1960) and support ships needed to support prolonged operations were simply not available. Secondly, decolonialisation made 'imperial policing' increasingly unrealistic and this, combined with financial weaknesses at home, made an East of Suez role ever more unattractive and unacceptable on political and economic grounds.

The naval problem that emerged from this was the identification of the carrier force with the East of Suez role; the British, because of their traditional role and the American underwriting of the West in general after 1945, having fallen into two fateful errors. Initially, British naval planning and doctrine failed to perceive that its aim might be to fight for the *use of the sea*. Secondly, the carriers themselves had not been maintained by regular construction and indeed no British carrier was laid down after 1945. Refitting and modernisation had been extensive and thorough, and the *Ark Royal* entered service in 1955 while the *Hermes* joined her four years later, both having been more than a decade on the stocks. But this was totally inadequate for the maintenance of effective carrier forces because the carriers in service were ageing and had to be struck off the lists at some time or another. If the British really intended to stay in the carrier business then the 1957 Review should have carried some immediate commitment to build, and the commitment was always being projected. Thus when the economy axe fell on the East of Suez role and the armed services generally in 1966-1967, the carriers naturally went to the block with it. The government of the day considered that the much talked-about replacement carrier, the CVA-01 with some 36 Phantoms and Buccaneers and eleven helicopters on about 55,000 tons, was both too weak and too expensive for a country apparently on its beam ends.

The ending of the East of Suez role and the cancellation of the CVA-01 project left the Royal Navy in very real danger of having no effective role for its surface ships because the foreshadowing of the end of British naval aviation came about at the same time as the *Styx* proved its effectiveness against the *Eliat*. Without carrier aviation the Royal Navy would be without a strike weapon and the subsequent introduction of the first guided weapons into the Royal Navy did not help matters. These were point defence weapons, designed to provide close-range self-defence which meant that Royal Navy ships had the means of defending themselves but almost no real capacity of operating offensively. The Royal Navy therefore found itself in a very difficult situation, though it did have the compensation in that it had secured the all-important strategic nuclear role. In 1962, under the terms of the Anglo-American Nassau Agreement, Britain secured access to American submarine, nuclear and missile technology, and this was to result in four SSBNs of the *Resolution*-class entering service by 1969.

The nuclear role was one that was unwanted by many naval officers because they feared that the cost of such a role would lead to the laying-up of surface units. In a sense such fears were confirmed, though it was really the general rise in the costs of ships and weapons rather than the *Polaris* programme as such that threatened the existence of the surface forces. The ending of the CVA-01 project compounded this problem in that it was intended that the phasing-out of the carriers by the mid-'seventies would be accompanied by the RAF providing air support for the fleet with long-range shore-based aircraft. The catch in this situation, of course, was that without carriers there could be no fleet, and the experience of the war had clearly been that shore-based aircraft were an invaluable supplement but not an effective substitute for integrated naval air power at sea.

It was this determination to retain some form of naval aviation plus the growth of the Soviet Navy that began to resolve the question of the future role of the Royal Navy because the Soviet Navy's development reconfirmed the importance of Britain's attempting to retain an oceanic

124

capability. It was recognised that Britain could no longer aspire to major status but it became increasingly important for her to be the leading contributor to a general European naval effort to support the Americans. In alliance terms it became vital for Britain to retain major naval forces in order to preserve British status, influence and power as West Germany began to clearly emerge as the most powerful of the European NATO states. With the British unable to match the Germans in military and economic power, the retention of substantial naval forces became important as a counter-balance to German power and pressure to secure command appointments. In both national and alliance terms it became ever more necessary for Britain to maintain oceanic naval forces for two further reasons. The French withdrawal from the integrated military command structure of NATO in 1966 left Britain with all the responsibility of leading the effort to ensure the security of the Channel and southern North Sea. The retention of significant surface forces was, moreover, ever more essential as a means of securing some degree of flexibility at a time when Alliance doctrine was changing from one of massive retaliation to flexible response. To surrender an oceanic role would entail leaving merchant shipping potentially vulnerable to some form of interference by an unfriendly power through an action short of war, with no means of either preventing this or retaliating. The retention of surface forces would at least deny others the opportunity of interfering with trade or some other aspect of peaceful maritime activity with complete impunity.

But the search for a settled role for the surface units became a long and protracted one that in the end revolved around a totally new concept, the 'Through Deck Cruiser'. The story of the TDC actually predates the 1966 decision to phase out the carriers. The realisation that the value of surface ships lay less in their organic weapons than in the helicopters they carried had led to proposals for a 6,000-ton cruiser, capable of operating nine Wessex A/S helicopters, to work with the fleet. The 1966 decision naturally increased interest in the idea, but it also altered it. Such a cruiser could no longer be a support for a carrier. In the absence of carriers such a cruiser had to be something rather special in that it would have to embrace a command role and air defence and anti-ship capabilities.

Some seven years were to elapse between the ending of the CVA-01 project and the ordering of the lead ship of a class of three, the *Invincible,* in 1973. In that time concept and designs underwent many changes that continued through building and trials before she was finally completed in June 1980. The *Invincible,* at 19,810 tons, is the largest British warship laid down since 1945 and her official designation (now changed to the dignity of a carrier) was CAH, Cruiser Assault Helicopter. This was, at one and the same time, both thoroughly misleading and a very accurate description.

In every sense she was a compromise between various conflicting influences. The Royal Navy was determined to stay in the naval aviation business, but the cost was prohibitive. The very mention of the word 'carrier' was anathema in the late 'sixties, hence the use of the label 'cruiser', but in her basic design the *Invincible* conformed to the lay-out of a carrier for the simple reason that a superstructure placed amidships with a flying-off platform aft represented a far less efficient use of space than a clear deck with offset island. As a result the TDC/CAH/CVL came to secure a 550-ft flight deck and an armament of five Sea Harrier V/STOL aircraft, nine Sea King A/S helicopters and a twin *Sea Dart* SAM system. It was planned to provide her with bow-mounted *Exocet* SSMs but this proposal was discarded with the final decision to equip her with Sea Harriers and because of the realisation that so large and expensive a ship - estimated to have cost in the end over £210,000,000 - simply could not afford to risk a SSM engagement with more heavily armed guided-missile warships. During construction the *Invincible* was modified to carry a marine unit and during trials was fitted with a 6½° ski-ramp. The third ship of the class, the *Ark Royal,* will have a purpose-built 15° ramp, and the significance of this development is that the performance of a Sea Harrier from a rolling start is greatly enhanced by its being launched up the 90-ft slope. Operating in a VTO role the Sea Harrier has a range of about 300 miles but in a STO role this is increased to nearly 500 miles. The ramp allows the Sea Harrier to carry nearly a 2,000-lb larger pay load than it would on a level launch.

The three *Invincibles* represent very cost-effective ships that reflect Britain's contracting naval power in the second half of the twentieth century. Their obvious weakness lies in their inability to keep pace with a fast task force and to carry out a proper air role in their own right, but in a supporting role and in covering replenishment groups, convoys and A/S forces they promise to be very useful ships, well suited to operate in a low-risk environment and in a sea control role. It seems quite possible that other nations may follow the British lead in this type of ship which does allow the smaller navies to retain some small capability in naval aviation without having to consider the vast expense of carriers. These ships, along with such roughly similar ships as Italy's *Garibaldi* and the *PA-11* of Spain, may well be one area where the European navies can provide a valuable supporting role for the Americans.

In the 'seventies the British also put in hand some twenty destroyers and seven frigates to replace such ageing classes as the *Tribal* and

Rothesay classes of frigates, and at the same time began the conversion of the 26-strong *Leanders* to carry either *Exocet* or *Ikara* missiles, depending on their designated role. But it is evident that though the Royal Navy has a settled role for its surface forces and has plans for new escorts and minehunters, the 'eighties may well prove to be a very difficult time for it. The essence of the difficulty is that whereas two decades ago equipment accounted for two-thirds of all defence expenditure, at the present time personnel costs now take up nearly half of total defence spending. Given the ever rising price of equipment and fuel and that all three services had to cut back their training programmes in 1980 to save money, it seems quite clear that with little prospect of real growth in the economy and little chance of inflation being reduced to very low levels, the stress on the procurement budget will remorselessly increase. The state of the economy is such that with very little prospect of any significant increase in defence spending in real terms some very hard inter-service and intra-service decisions will have to be taken over the next few years, if only because in 1980 the decision was taken to replace the old *Polaris* submarines with *Trident* SSBNs. The whole *Trident* programme has been costed at about £5,000 million at 1980 prices, and this represents 63 per cent of the entire defence budget for FY 80. Even allowing for the fact that building will have to spread over several years because of limited construction facilities, the peak building years will absorb 10 per cent of the present-level procurement budget. If the intention to retain a strategic nuclear deterrent through the *Trident* programme is to be turned into reality, therefore, it would seem that unless defence spending is substantially increased high-cost programmes for the conventional forces will have to be cut - and the Royal Navy and RAF would be very vulnerable because of the high costs and long lead times of their procurement programmes. In this case the RAF because its contribution to overall NATO capabilities is relatively smaller, may prove to be the more vulnerable, but the Navy's position is exposed since the latest Type 42 *Sheffield*-class destroyers were costed in the present estimates at £85 million each and the last of the *Broadswords* are certain to cost more than £100 million. The three new *Trafalgar*-class SSNs will each cost an estimated £175 million and even a 615-ton *Hunt*-class coastal minehunter will cost over £25 million. The vulnerability of future programmes is clear, and how the problem of cost is to be overcome is equally unclear. This financial problem is one that is not confined to Britain since it was a general one that affects all NATO members in one way or another - but the Americans do have special difficulties of their own.

The Royal Navy and the French Navy, indeed all the navies of the European NATO powers, are marginal in themselves to the balance of power at sea. The combined strength is substantial and in numbers alone European NATO navies (including France) just about match Soviet sea-going forces in the European theatre. But in terms of quality, homogeneity and sheer striking power the backbone of the alliance is the American IInd (Atlantic) and VIth (Mediterranean) Fleets. Only the US Navy has any chance of effectively defending the sea-borne lines of communication on which the North Atlantic alliance depends.

American ability to defend these lines of communication, however, has been increasingly questioned, not because of any doubt about American resolution or professionalism but because of lack of strength. The 'seventies began with the US Navy possibly at the peak of its post-war power. The Vietnam war resulted in a great swelling of American naval power as carriers, escorts, assault ships and riverine craft were reactivated and put back into service. The conversion of eight boats of the *Lafayette*-class of SSBN to *Polaris A-3* missiles by 1970 meant that all 31 of the *Lafayette* and *Benjamin Franklin* classes were equipped with a weapon far superior to the *Polaris A-2,* thereby ensuring the security and viability of the American strategic deterrent. With three new nuclear-powered carriers in the pipeline the US Navy was seemingly well placed, even though the Soviet Navy's deployment was clearly more than casual.

The 'seventies, however, proved a very difficult and troubled decade for the US Navy because of the combination of political upheaval and uncertainty with inflation and recession. These hit the Navy when it was in a transitional phase. There was one problem that it faced at the beginning of the decade that has gradually assumed increasingly serious dimensions during the 'seventies and which has not been properly resolved. This problem affected most parts of the Navy, but two of its branches, the carriers and the strategic submarines, were most seriously affected, and it is on these two branches that our attention will be directed. The problem, in short, was block obsolescence at a time when mounting costs made replacement very difficult.

Probably the most seriously affected was the submarine arm because at the present time it carries 55 per cent of all the warheads in the US strategic arsenal and the invulnerability and continued deployment of the nineteen *Lafayettes,* twelve *Franklins,* five *Ethan Allens* and five *George Washingtons* are critical to the maintenance of the strategic nuclear balance. To put the problem in its simplest form, the USA secured an overwhelming strategic advantage over the USSR in the ten years between 1965 and 1975 because of the crash construction programmes of the early 'sixties. The last of these boats, the *Will Rogers,* entered service in April 1967 while the first, the *George Washington* herself, was commissioned in December 1959. By 31 December 1983 sixteen American SSBNs would have been in service for more than twenty years, and if none were struck from the lists all would be into their third decade of service by 1987. They have to replaced because invariably they wear out, and given the cost of the new *Ohio* class and, more critically, the fact that with the Newport News Yard in Virginia committed to CVN construction only one yard, the General Electric Yard at Groton in Connecticut, can build such complicated weapons systems, there are very real fears for the security of the submarine deterrent over the next ten to fifteen years.

Obsolescence of design permits no sentimentality and respects no reputations, and the fact that the *George Washington* was the first submarine to fire a strategic missile while submerged (20 July 1960) is to her detriment. She and her four sisters, three of them authorised in FY 58 and two converted from previously ordered SSNs, all carry *Polaris A-3,* but no attempt will be made to prolong their service life. All entered service before March 1961 and are simply too old to permit modification. Similarly, the *Ethan Allens,* four of which were ordered in FY 59 and the last in FY 61, are not to be converted.

The *Lafayettes* and *Franklins,* which are basically the same class except for the fact that the latter are quieter, were all ordered between 1961 and 1965, and all were converted between 1970 and 1978 to carry sixteen UGM-73A *Poseidon C-3* missiles. This represented a considerable increase in the offensive power of these 31 boats. The early *Polaris* marks had been single-head missiles, the *A-3* being a MRV with three warheads patterned to straddle a target in a 'footprint'. The *Poseidon* was MIRVed, with each of its ten warheads to 5,120, but this increase, entirely confined to these two classes, did not alter the fact that the *Lafayettes* and *Franklins* were stable mates of the *Allens* and *George Washingtons,* and that the last to be converted, the *Daniel Webster,* was fourteen years old when her refit was completed. Updating the weapons systems could not bring back lost youth.

In 1974 the US Navy made the proposal to build ten new *Ohio*-class SSBNs, each armed with 24 UGM-96A *Trident C-4* missiles (normally called the *Trident I*) over four years. It was also proposed to convert twelve of the later *Poseidon* submarines to take the new missile. But there were formidable obstacles in the way of both proposals. Conversion, though less extensive than the upgrading from *Polaris* to *Poseidon,* would remain expensive because of the need to drastically modify the fire control, instrumentation and missile checkout systems. The cost would be high, but the process would be relatively quick - about fifteen months - and this was certainly not the case with purpose-built *Trident* submarines. To carry 24 *Tridents* 18,700 tons of submarine, with a larger power pack, were needed, and it was small wonder that the Americans looked around for smaller and cheaper SSBNs. Inevitably none were to be found. The stuttering SALT negotiations, with the uncertainty of just what would finally be allowed the Americans under a second arms limitation treaty, did not help resolve or hasten decisions, and in 1978 the original proposal was watered down to ten in eight years, the last two being projected for FY 84.

Not surprisingly some disquiet has been expressed about this programme, mainly on two counts. Firstly, it put a lot of very large and expensive eggs in a very small number of baskets. Secondly, a very complicated technical argument surrounded the *Trident* missile. While it outranged the SS-N-6 carried in Soviet *Yankee*-class SSBMs, it was outranged by the SS-N-8 carried by the *Delta II* class. Neither the SS-N-6 nor the SS-N-8 were MIRVed, but the SS-N-18, carried by the latest *Delta III* class of Soviet SSBMs was MIRVed, though it is believed to carry fewer warheads than the *Trident I*. The *Trident I,* however, does not outrange the SS-N-18, and though in time the *Trident I* is due to be MARVed and subsequently replaced in service by the 6,000-mile MARVed *Trident II,* there is no guarantee that the latter will re-establish American technical superiority over the Soviets - and it is not certain that the *Trident II* programme will be developed. The cause of American uneasiness about this complicated set of facts was a dislike of being qualitatively inferior in any way to a numerically superior opponent. Behind all these considerations, moreover, is the lurking fear that the much talked-about breakthrough in ASW might become reality. Whether this would favour the numerically superior or the numerically inferior is speculative, but it is certainly something that must disturb the sleep of submarine Flag Officers in many countries.

In the field of carrier development the 'seventies was an even more traumatic time for the US Navy as it faced up to the reality that its old carriers of World War II vintage had to be phased out of service as they, too, began to approach the end of their working lives with nothing to replace them. At the present time the US Navy has thirteen carriers, all but two of them post-war vintage, with the *Coral Sea,* less her air group held in reserve, the *Lexington* detailed for training duties and the *Carl Vinson* being built. Six other carriers are laid up. This total represents the lowest number of carriers in American service since the start of the Korean war, and by the 'nineties the Americans plan to operate a twelve-carrier fleet.

In the course of the 'seventies successive presidents, defence secretaries, Congresses and naval commanders tied themselves into knots over problems that really boiled down to one thing - dollars. Not even the Americans, with all their wealth, could afford to be complacent about the remorseless rise in the cost of ships, especially when the *Vinson* clearly threatened to break the $2,000 million barrier, even without her air group. Given that the carrier had to be built around her air group which had to be a balanced force of fighter (Phantoms/Tomcats) squadrons, light (Corsairs) and medium (Intruders) attack squadrons and anti-submarine Sea King helicopters and Vikings, plus various detachments of reconnaissance, ECM, early warning and refuelling aircraft, rising costs were killing the carrier. It was small wonder, therefore, that rising costs plus an eight-year lead time in construction forced the US Navy to look round for something that would be more cost-effective.

This search was urgent. The oldest of the large fleet carriers, the *Midways,* were no longer capable of operating a complete air group and they were in effect World War II ships though they entered service just too late to see action in the Pacific. The *Franklin D. Roosevelt* was struck in 1977, and the two remaining ships of the class were obviously not going to last beyond the mid-'eighties. The four *Forrestal* carriers, laid down between 1952 and 1955 represented a considerable qualitative advance on the *Midways,* but time has now eroded this. The Americans were therefore faced with the same problem of block obsolescence with their carriers as they were with their SSBNs. To get around the difficulty the Navy wanted another CVN and to take the remaining carriers one by one out of service for major reconstruction (called Service Life Extension Programmes) in order to keep twelve continually in service until about the year 2000. The immediate problem, however, was that as a result of a high rate of domestic inflation, various labour, construction and design problems and restricted means of production, carriers were pricing themselves out of reach, even though everyone agreed that there was no real substitute for them.

But, as noted, the fleet carrier problem was only one aspect of the overall carrier difficulty. In 1968 the US Navy had eleven CVS, all of them *Essex*-class carriers from World War II in service, and these had to go. In fact by 1974 they had gone, and there was no clear idea as to what would come in their place. American planners had long since made one important decision. This was to minimise the cost of any replacement and to make a clear distinction between CVS replacements and the larger, heavier and more costly fleet units. By about 1970 American thought had turned to the idea of the DDH, a destroyer with helicopters, but as the British were finding at the same time, at least 8,000 tons of warship were needed to carry such large helicopters as the Sea King. By May 1971 when the Americans came up with the designation Sea Control

131

Ship (SCS), their thoughts had turned to a small multi-purpose carrier, suspiciously like the British *Invincible* which was under consideration at this time. Perhaps it was such a similarity that led to the SCS concept being viewed with such suspicion in many quarters, but after a series of trials on the *Guam* between 1972 and 1974, the US Navy seemed to be very much in favour of a 14,000-ton ship with a speed of 26 knots and a mixed air group of between twelve and eighteen aircraft, up to six of them V/STOL and the remainder Sea King A/S helicopters. The SCS concept envisaged such ships operating in a sea control role, supporting amphibious assaults, providing close air support, conducting mine warfare and generally operating in a low-risk environment.

When the SCS concept was mooted as a serious proposition in 1973 the US Navy was thinking in terms of up to twenty such ships, and it was determined to keep unit costs under $100 million, less the lead ship. But the whole of the SCS concept was abhorrent to Congress. What the US Navy was trying to do in effect was to secure a low-cost second-class replacement for light and anti-submarine carriers but which could not keep pace with a task force and could not operate in the face of real danger. After funding the research and design project in 1973 Congress threw out the notion in 1975 on the grounds that such ships were not cost-effective and out of place for an oceanic navy. With the Navy in 1975 seeking just three such ships and wanting about $185 million for FY 75 for just the lead ship, the hostility of Congress merely on economic grounds alone was perhaps understandable. Yet there were certain other objections that were probably more important to the project being shelved. In the eyes of her detractors a SCS was not sufficiently strong in offensive power - how a V/STOL aircraft was to perform an interceptor role against high-altitude and/or supersonic aircraft was never explained - and it became clear that Congress would never sanction a ship that could be seen as a tacit step towards second-class status.

The US Navy, however, still remained convinced of the value of such ships. In the face of a growing submarine, surface and air threat to its freedom of movement, it had moved away from the notion of absolute command of the sea, as it had until very recently enjoyed, in favour of the idea of sea control. This meant effectively controlling critically important sea areas, usually for limited periods of time, in order to deny an enemy use of them, and pessimists were already talking in terms of being able to do no more at sea than attempting to deny the Soviet Navy access into the North Atlantic. Such views cast very real doubts over American ability to get convoys through to western Europe. The Americans were committed to the 'roll-over' concept, the notion that when faced with a mid-Atlantic threat, American task forces, rather like convoys with escort carriers in the war, would 'roll-over' the opposition by fighting for and winning control of the seas through which it passed. To make such an idea work numbers were important, and the SCS concept, though weak in offensive power, was not unreasonable since ships would provide a platform for a considerable number of helicopters, the most potent threat to nuclear-powered submarines. Obviously there were various objections to the whole theory of sea control and 'roll-over'. The analogy with escort carriers with convoys in the Second World War was not an exact one since the ability of escort carriers during the war to control the seas around a convoy was but one part of the process whereby escorts fought for and secured a general command of the seas. The balance between escorts and submarines, moreover, had shifted in favour of submarines because of the introduction of nuclear propulsion for submarines, the greater destructiveness of their weapons and their superior acquisition ranges. The helicopter being the all-important exception, submarines could outrun escorts. But these points and the objections of Congress in no way deflected the US Navy from its wish for a SCS. Because it retained confidence both in the SCS concept and in V/STOL aircraft operating at sea, the US Navy came up with three sets of plans for some form of ASW carrier. Firstly, it retained its original SCS concept. Secondly, it proposed a V/STOL (or Vistol) Support Ship (VSS) of 22,000 tons and thirdly it suggested a 33,000-ton VSS with two catapults and upwards of fifty aircraft.

By formulating ideas for this third type of ship the US Navy, unfortunately for itself, began to move into another area of development and investigation. In July 1975 Defence Secretary Schlesinger, seriously alarmed about the rising costs of the *Nimitz* class, directed the Navy to consider medium-sized alternatives to the giant carriers. The alternatives were to be nuclear-powered and capable of operating with the fleet carriers. The term 'medium-sized' seems to have been taken with a large measure of salt because the suggestions that the Navy came up with involved the smallest of the three CVV possibilities weighing in at 64,000 tons (deep load) and the largest at 84,000 tons. The smallest version was set to carry between 48 and 53 aircraft, and both the larger versions were to have between 59 and 65.

The great advantage of such ships would have been their relative economy in manpower (crews of up to 3,800 instead of the 6,000 of the *Nimitz*) and their possession of very substantial strike forces. But when it came to looking closely at the details various serious objections emerged. It became apparent that to design a CVV from scratch would work out as expensive as building to a settled CVN blueprint. Moreover, in size, the heaviest of the CVVs would be very little different from the last of the conventionally-powered carriers, the *John F. Kennedy.* Not surprisingly, therefore, the Navy settled for building a fourth *Nimitz,* and it marshalled a formidable array of evidence to support its case. A CVV would take longer to design and build than another CVN, and prove just as expensive, and with two catapaults and sixty aircraft would be considerably inferior to the *Kennedy* with four catapaults and 84 aircraft. What the Navy probably thought would be the clinching argument in favour of another CVN was the view that there would seem little justification for building just one CVV. With a lead ship costing at least $2,000 million there was no point in building just one because unit costs would only be brought down if others followed her, and there seemed little point in building a number of CVVs if this entailed the gradual reduction of the number of heavier carriers in service. Indeed, from the mid-'seventies onwards the large carriers began conversion to carry their own ASW force, so that it would seem that the US Navy was pushing a concept that could not possibly be accepted.

Congress, in voting the appropriations for FY 78, accepted this logic and voted funds for another CVN, but President Carter, carrying on where he left off with the B-1 bomber, the ERW project and the *Ohio*-class programme, killed the bill (just as he did the hovercraft ACV/SES programmes) and subsequently insisted upon the construction of one CVV of 62,427 tons (deep load) with a 55/65-strong air group. In its turn this was rejected by Congress, and after the administration had had the proposal for another *Kennedy* disregarded by Congress, Carter finally sanctioned the inclusion of a fourth *Nimitz* in the FY 80 defence budget. In this manner the US Navy finally secured its extra carrier, but some six years after its initial request had been made and, as it transpired, without any form of compensation for the loss of time and fighting power in the form of a SCS, VSS or CVV. Though the US Navy secured the carrier that will enable it to function as a twelve-carrier force, the process was a slow and painful one. Just how the Navy will fare under the Reagan administration is mere conjecture, but there can be no getting away from the fact that even if new contracts were placed on inauguration day, large surface units thus ordered would probably not see service in the 'eighties. What has happened in the late 'sixties and the 'seventies, in both the carrier and SSBN branches, has not been particularly important in the short term, but will have serious implications for the 'nineties when the whole of the US Navy will be more than slightly rheumatic.

CHAPTER VI

THE BALANCE OF POWER

As one looks back over the pages of the preceeding chapter one cannot help but note their sombre tone, and it would be all too easy to look at numbers and types and see in them the yardstick of naval power. It would be equally easy to see in recent developments western confusion and irresolution and compare this to the seemingly inexorable growth on the part of a Soviet Navy whose intentions seem hardly likely to be benign.

In the examination of the development of the Soviet Navy earlier pages have attempted to offer possible explanations of events that are subject to several interpretations and much polemic. The text has tried to do so in as uncontroversial a manner as possible in order to set events against historical perspective and to ensure that the view of sea power in the 'eighties is reasoned and balanced. Certain corrections remain to be made, however, to complete the process.

Firstly, to return to a point made earlier about the Imperial German Navy, ships and even fleets can be built in a matter of years, but navies cannot. Naval tradition and experience cannot be built up without war, and the Soviet Navy has little combat experience and it has no history or practical knowledge of conducting sustained operations on the high seas. Various exercises in the 'seventies have shown that the Soviet Navy has a capability in all the world's oceans and that in many aspects of technique, particularly RAS, it has made fast and considerable progress. Yet even in a push-button age the newness of the Soviet Navy makes it an unknown quality. As such it has to be treated with respect because it is always prudent to assume ability on the part of the unknown rather than to undervalue it, but at the same time America battle technique, so amply demonstrated by carrier operations in the South China Sea during the Vietnam war, must always be counted on the western side. The growth and sheer size of the Soviet Navy must take account of the fact that the Soviets are always loathe to discard anything that may prove of value, and keep a high proportion of even quite new ships in reserve. The ships that come out are invariably the same ones time after time, and even if the others are kept in a high state of readiness, much time would have to elapse before they could get to sea. Soviet strength, moreover, must always be assessed by its division into four separate areas of interest.

Secondly, however alarming the state of western society may appear at any given moment, and however tempting the notion that the grass is always greener on the other (Soviet) side of the hill may be, the Soviet Union has problems of her own. It is altogether wrong to see the state of East-West relations in terms of the East being strong and the West being weak though there is no doubting the fact that the Soviet Union is in military terms the most powerful state on the planet. But this has only been achieved at a frightful distortion of the Soviet economy. In Soviet eyes time is not necessarily on their side. Though Marxist economic determinism foreshadows the destruction of capitalism as inevitable, the same Marxist analysis gives victory in war to the side that is the economically stronger - and that is not the Soviet bloc. Moreover, in immediate terms of Soviet domestic politics, the Soviet leadership has problems that make some of those of the West seem not too severe in comparison. The Soviets have an open-ended commitment to support the crippling liabilities of Cuba and Vietnam, and have found themselves committed to politically and financially ruinous actions in Kampuchea and Afghanistan. Soviet agriculture is not too far removed from being a disaster area and the bulk of Soviet industry is in urgent and drastic need of decentralisation and massive investment. Yet the advantages of concentrated power are too tempting to those that hold it to allow its dilution at a time when the Kremlin still sees the USSR as a revolutionary bastion surrounded by enemies. Seen from Moscow the world still presents many opportunities but also many dangers. The forces of the North Atlantic Alliance remain very powerful, and we are apt to forget how powerful they are in defensive terms. Since it is the West's intention to deter possible Soviet aggression by ensuring that the price of aggression would be excessive, deterrence enforces uncertainty on the part of the Soviets at the very time when they are approaching their optimum strength. The Soviet Union spreads itself across 170° of longitude, eleven time zones, and in the west it faces more sophisticated opponents and in the east an opponent with a 4:1 numerical advantage and increasingly sophisticated economy. The Soviet defence problem begins to assume nightmarish proportions when it is remembered that the Soviet birthrate as a whole is low and that there is a considerable imbalance within it between the Russian and non-Russian parts of the population. (By the year 2000 it has been suggested that the country with the greatest number of Moslems after Indonesia will be the USSR).

In the mid-'eighties the Soviets will stand at the peak of their military strength and thereafter will operate on a declining scale of military effectiveness as the low Soviet birthrate, western sophistication and Chinese advances begin to erode Soviet superiority. Whether this would be a destabilising element or a factor that would induce caution on the part of the USSR is a moot point, but it is easy to believe that at the present time there is a substantial body of opinion in the Soviet military and political leadership that believes that the Soviet Union is faced with the 'Go now or never' alternative. France in 1870 and Austria-Hungary in 1914 are examples of states that chose war as the means of ensuring their great power status at a time when they were in relative decline compared to their opponents. There is an obvious parallel with the Soviet Union today.

Thirdly, though the West is beset with long-term problems, over the last two decades its building has generally matched that of the Soviets. In the field of modern ship construction the Soviets have not achieved a clear cut advantage of numbers over the Americans though they do have a marginal advantage of relative geographical concentration and far fewer oceanic interests to defend. In overall numbers, however, the Soviets hold several advantages, and given the fact that the Soviet Navy is largely made up of 'first-shot, one-shot' ships, the importance of the older ships of lesser fighting value will be out of all proportion to their relative value in the event of the modern ships of the two sides cancelling one another out. The Soviets regard their ships as expendable because there are no absolutely critical oceanic interests which have to be defended. Unlike western states that live by the sea there is nothing at sea that is non-negotiable for the Soviets. They can afford losses if this ensures the neutralisation of western naval power whereas western navies have to remain intact in order to retain the use of the sea.*

Yet here is the paradox of naval power in the 'eighties. The importance of the sea, as a means of transport, as a source of food, and for its mineral resources, has probably never been greater than it is at the present time. As pressure on resources continues to grow this importance will increase. At the present time the major naval powers of the world are engaged in a quantitative and qualitative arms race the cost of which probably makes it the most expensive in history, yet never has their ability to command the sea been smaller. Despite expenditure of money

---

* The basic statement that the Soviet ships are 'first-shot, one-shot' vessels is one that needs some qualification. In historical terms this is certainly true, but modern Soviet ships are increasingly being configured to survive and fight for longer periods. In this respect the *Kirov* is an obvious example of this trend. Being so large and stable a weapons platform she has a considerable reload capacity, and is able to carry ordnance safe from the elements. But because of the Soviet Navy's long tail of older ships, the basic premise remains true, at least for the moment.

and ingenuity on an almost prohibitive scale, navies no longer think in terms of commanding or using the sea: at the very best they think in terms of denying an enemy access to certain parts of it for certain periods of time. Yet even this ability, so dubious an asset in so many ways, is an essential one because given the commitment to policies of deterrence and the existence of American and Soviet nuclear arsenals that are sufficient to inflict mutually assured destruction in the event of their use, surface ships retain a flexibility and an importance that land and air forces do not possess. This has to be maintained if nations are to escape the dilemma President Kennedy referred to in his inaugural address in 1961 - the choice between suicide and surrender. Only through conventional strength can there be the flexibility to give an option other than nuclear exchange; surface naval forces will assume an ever greater importance in this role, just as they will remain, along with all the other elements of sea power, vital not merely in the projection of power beyond national frontiers but in ensuring the prosperity of all those who use the sea in peace.

Comparative Strengths in February 1980 of the Soviet, American, European NATO and Canadian Navies, excluding ships in reserve, building and projected.

	USSR	USA	FRANCE	UK	WEST GERMANY	ITALY
SSBN	71	41	5	4		
SSB	19					
SSGN	45					
SSG	23					
SSN	49	75		12		
SS	148	7	19	16	25	10
CV/CVN		13				
CVV			2			
CVV (Other)				1		
CVS	2			1		
ASW Cruiser/CVL	2		1	2	1	
CG (Heavy)	1					
CG/CGN	28	26	1	7		2
DDG	33	63	18	7	7	4
DD	51	33	1		4	3
FFG	28	54	8	32		4
FF	113	13	13	13	6	10
Corvette (G)	58					
Corvette					6	8
FAC (All Types)	297		5		40	7
Patrol Craft	169	65	18	19		
MCM oceanic	144	25	5			4
MCM other	231		20	29	60	36
Amphibious	128	154	53	68	22	58
Hydrofoils	122	1		6		2
Support Ships	241	114	27	43	22	7
Miscellaneous	720	1183	158	207	99	149
Manpower in '000s	433	709	69	68	38	41

GREECE AND TURKEY	PORTUGAL	CANADA
25	3	3
		4
24		19
6	17	
45		
56	27	13
48	4	
170	15	
	6	10
31		1
72	4	40
69	14	15

NOTES TO TABLES

1.   The two remaining members of NATO, Iceland and Luxembourg, do not possess naval forces.

2.   The figures have been compiled from data drawn from the current editions of *Jane's Fighting Ships, The Military Balance* and *The Strategic Survey*. Because of the impossibility of reconciling and standardising different national classifications, all the figures in the table, but particularly those relating to escorts and ships of lesser value, are subject to dispute. The information provided in the tables remains, however, correct in general terms.

3.   Excluded from the lists are
   (a)   for the USA four battleships and two heavy cruisers held in reserve
   (b)   for the USSR twelve light cruisers of the *Sverdlov* class and the *Komsomolets* because of their uncertain classification and operational status. The *Sverdlovs* vary between command ships, guided weapons cruisers and orthodox 6-in cruisers.

4.   The word "hydrofoil" in this instance includes ACV/SES.

5.   Naturally excluded from the lists are carriers held by other navies. Argentina, Australia, Brazil and India each retain a single carrier, all of them ex-British light carriers of WW2-vintage. Those in South American employment saw service in the Pacific in 1945.

Key to abbreviations:-

SS:	Submarine	ASW:	Anti-submarine Warfare
N:	Nuclear-powered	DD:	Destroyer
CVS:	Anti-submarine carrier	MCM:	Anti-mine ship
C:	Cruiser	G:	Guided Weapons
FAC:	Fast Attack Craft	CVV:	Medium carrier
B:	Ballistic Missile	CVL:	Light carrier
CV:	Heavy carrier	FF:	Frigate

EPILOGUE

ADMIRAL OF THE FLEET THE LORD HILL NORTON, G.C.B.

The excellent, in-depth, analysis in the preceeding chapters brings us right up to date with the developments of the navies of the Soviet Union and the West, and deals carefully and accurately with the warships themselves and with their weapons systems. Some unsettling questions must be left in the minds of his readers about where this may all lead, in times of rising tension or actual hostilities between the two blocs. Will there be a war at sea? What, indeed, may happen at sea should war come? An attempt will be made in what follows, drawing on Mr Willmott's admirable background, if not to answer the question in definitive terms (I am not in the prophecy business), at least to indicate some tentative conclusions, on the evidence.

We need to think first, and also probably last, of the main maritime objectives of the two sides in the East/West confrontation; to think of what each has to risk, and whether the means of achieving and safe-guarding those objectives are adequate; or if not, in which respects they can be seen to fall short. It must be emphasised at the outset, that for the purposes of this essay consideration will be given to war at sea, which does not form part of general nuclear war and which would last for some weeks or even months, rather than days. It would not necessarily be connected with a simultaneous land-air campaign in Europe, though it could well be that either or both sides have recourse to maritime nuclear weapons. For those who may think this an improbable scenario, it may (or may not) suffice to say that the author does not. If collateral for this personal view is needed, it is an historic fact that in the Second World War the battles at sea raged for seven months before the clash on land began in earnest, and, secondly, nuclear weapons used at sea involve none of the horrors of mass destruction, no collateral damage on an unimaginable scale, which would follow their use on, or over, land.

To consider, then, the objectives of both sides, which in itself would be a study of some magnitude and detail, it can fairly be asserted - and Mr Willmott correctly does so - that naval warfare is today (and probably always has been) about control of sea-borne lines of communication. This lies at the very heart of what will be fought for in any future war at sea.

The seas are of infinitely more importance to the NATO Allies than they are to the Soviets, because it is along Conrad's great highways that their energy, raw materials and much of their food travels to North America and to Western Europe in peace. Any interruption of that truly vital trade would bring their industry (and not just their Defence industries) to a halt very quickly, as well as making all their peoples cold, dark and hungry. To give some perspective to this assertion, by way of just one example, over one billon tons of crude oil were imported into NATO countries by sea in 1978 alone. In military terms it is the integrity of the 'Atlantic Bridge', for the supply, re-inforcement, and re-supply of Europe from North America upon which the whole of NATO's deterrent strategy depends - and both sides know it. This, very starkly, is what the West has at risk, and from which, broadly and simply, their primary objective can at once be discerned: to keep these highways and that bridge open to traffic in both directions. The Soviets, by contrast, have no such need of sea-borne trade either for their economy or for their war-machine. Their primary objective can be readily perceived, and also amounts to no more and no less than to cut the sea-borne lanes of communication upon which the West so critically depends.

To what extent, we must now enquire, does each side possess (or lack) the means to achieve these simply stated, but crucial, objectives?

Can the Soviet Navy, as constituted, throttle our very means of livelihood? Can it, if war comes, break the Atlantic Bridge and so destroy at a stroke the very heart of NATO's deterrent posture in Europe?

Let us look more closely, and specifically, at these two related tasks. In material terms Mr Willmott has shown the sheer size and diversity of the Soviet fleet. Observation of their activities by the West has been close and continuous since the threat became clear. Particularly dramatic examples were the world-wide exercises code-named (in the West) OKEAN '70 and '75, when some hundreds of warships of all types were successfully deployed and controlled from Moscow. The ships themselves, apart from their sheer numbers, are well built and well armed, though by Western naval standards extremely uncomfortable for their ships' companies (which could affect any but a fairly short campaign). Their weapons, especially guided missiles for air defence and surface attack are excellent, and almost certainly superior to those in Allied navies. There is, of course, a good reason for this, in their early recognition of the powerful threat posed by the American attack carrier battle groups and the modest British components of them. These are, demonstrably, now much reduced and, further, the first Soviet aircraft carriers are now themselves coming forward, ironically at the same time as the British have been forced by economy to abandon theirs. But although the 'old school' have won the all-arms, balanced fleet, argument it is far from clear to a critical professional eye that they have got the balance right for their particular task.

There is, however that may be in general, hardly any doubt that the Soviet submarine fleet is formidable by any standards. Not less than 300 of these vessels, of which probably nearly one-third is nuclear-powered, are now deployed, and one may reasonably compare that number with the 50 much slower, shallower, diesel-electric submersibles with which Grand Admiral Döenitz started his assault on the Atlantic Bridge (or lifeline) in 1939. If we reflect on what has here been described as the primary objective - indeed the secondary objectives too - of the Soviet Navy it must be seen that in their submarine arm must lie their gravest threat to us, and the greatest hope of success for them. It is strange, and perhaps useful collateral for Mr Willmott's assessment just quoted, that possibly the most obvious weakness of the Soviet Navy is in anti-submarine warfare. It is generally held by objective observers that they are well behind the West in this field, which must bear considerable weight in the balance we are attempting to strike, though there can be no room for complacency in this - or any other maritime - matter when the speed of Soviet technical advance in so many other fields is borne in mind.

Another element to be considered when seeking to establish the extent to which the Soviet Navy can achieve its aims, is that of maritime air power. Until their large aircraft carriers are proven in service, which will not be for some time yet, they have relied on their very large shore-based naval air arm, and whether their carriers are successful or not they will inevitably continue to do so. This large force has demonstrated its ability to cover all those seas and oceans through which the Western lifelines pass, and the aircraft are lavishly equipped for maritime reconnaissance, and equally well armed for offensive anti-ship operations. There is no comparable shore-based maritime air power in the West, and as has already been noted, Allied aircraft carrier numbers have seriously declined. Nor should the constantly orbiting radar ocean reconnaissance satellites, against which there is at present no counter, be left out of the tally of Soviet strength.

If we may turn from the broad sweep of Soviet *machtpolitik,* and from the tangible ships and aircraft and their weapons systems as a means of making it good, to the aptitude of the Soviet sailors for a war at sea, a less impressive, and correspondingly less daunting, picture quickly emerges. The Russians have certainly had a long naval tradition, but it is not bred in the bone of that vast country, where only a tiny proportion of the population has ever actually seen the sea. The Bear is a land animal even if, as it is now fashionable in naval circles to say, he has learned to swim. It must be supposed, on grounds of age alone, that none of the officers and men in the Soviet Navy have ever been in action at sea; and for those still in business at the top, their memories of the ultimate test of aptitude can only be of their disastrous failures in the Second World War, briefly but adequately documented in chapter V. It is generally accepted that there can be no substitute for combat experience, however thorough and well planned peace time training, even in major exercises, may be. For this reason alone it is not erring on the side of under-estimating the opposition, to assume that the performance of the Soviet fleet, whether deployed in task groups or in single units, will fall short of that of the Allied navies with a much more recent (for example in Korea and Vietnam) and a much more successful, track record over many years. At the same time, it must be admitted that the morale of the ordinary Russian sailor is high, over-worked conscript though he may be. When Admiral Sir Ray Lygo was commanding the *Ark Royal* she collided with a shadowing Soviet destroyer and he was appalled to find that 'when we were trying to fish Russian sailors out of the sea, they would rather risk drowning than be rescued by us.'

My own view is that whatever the merits of the ordinary seaman, the leadership will react less well and recover less quickly when events do not go according to plan. If this be true it is a fortunate historical fact that hardly any battle has ever gone according to plan.

To turn at once and examine the other side of the equation is, by now, a somewhat shorter and simpler task. Our own objectives are in many respects more straightforward and our strengths and weaknesses are better known. The attempt to put some flesh on the bare bones of whether NATO has the maritime power to meet its primary objective of keeping the Atlantic Bridge open, and more generally whether the West is capable of keeping open the sea lanes, must nevertheless be made.

To deal first with numbers, it can be said at once that it is at sea, and only at sea, that the West today is in the broadest sense still superior to the Soviets, despite the constant preoccupation - amounting almost to hypnosis - of the European Allies with the land-air balance in their Central Region. But it is undoubtedly more difficult to compare numbers on, over and under the sea in a meaningful way, partly because types of both warships and their offensive and defensive weapons differ more markedly than they do on land or in the air, and partly because the in-fluence of the tangibles and intangibles is much more pronounced at sea. It is generally accepted, as a base line, that the NATO navies together outnumber those of the Soviets (and even those of the Warsaw Pact, for the Polish and East German navies are far from insignificant). A detailed catalogue would not contribute much to an understanding of the whole maritime balance, but the tonnage of NATO navies is a good deal greater, they have at least six times the number of attack aircraft carriers, an advantage of perhaps one and a half times in number of ships of frigate size and above. On the other hand the Soviet Navy has rather more nuclear powered attack submarines and at least five times as many diesel-electric submarines (though many of these are obsolescent), and about ten times more land-based maritime aircraft, with a similar ratio, in reverse, afloat. Finally, and merely for the record, the number of sailors deployed in the maritime balance shows a ratio of about seven to four in favour of the West. If these ratios are then re-calculated to include the navies of traditionally pro-Western countries, as for example, Japan, Australia and New Zealand, South Africa and the South Americas, the balance of men and material on a straight head-count, tips even more clearly against the Soviets. It must, of course, be understood that the United States Navy is the backbone, and by far the greatest strength of the Allied (and Western) naval order of battle, and its actual and future power requires some qualification, as will be shown shortly. The simple numerical comparison may be rounded off with a feature of some surprise, in the light of all that has been observed and written about the astounding expansion of the Soviet Navy in the last 15-20 years: the rate of construction of all types, with the sole exception of nuclear powered (and nuclear armed) submarines, in the Allied and Western navies has been, type for type, broadly in line with that achieved - at unparalleled economic and social sacrifice - by Gorshkov. It has been calculated, however, that on present trends (and unreplaced obsolescence is possibly the most important) even this basic numerical balance could have shifted markedly in favour of the Soviets by, say, 1995 - and this could well have a strong influence on 'what will happen'.

To add an essential gloss to this excursion into numbers due account must also be taken of the ratio of offensive to defensive forces in naval warfare. It has been established for many years that in a land-air war in Europe an attacker (or aggressor) must be able to count upon a general superiority of three to one in men, and all the engines of war they man and fight, to have any real confidence of success. This ratio, commonly known as the Lidell Hart factor after its first propounder, can obviously be varied up or down by surprise, or concentration, greater skill, better weapons, better leadership or tactics, and other variables mostly intangible. But at sea hardly any of these apply and those that do have much less force because the 'battlefield' is infinitely larger, is three rather than two-dimensional, and has no boundaries, natural obstacles (except the.

land), nor advantages of terrain. So not only does the Liddell-Hart ratio have no relevance to the war at sea, but the entire operational experience of both the First and Second World Wars has conclusively shown that it is actually sharply reversed, and that the defence of shipping requires much larger forces than those of the attacker. No comparable rule of thumb ratio has evolved which is of general application partly because of simple geography, and partly because the control or denial of particular sea areas may be hindered or helped by varying surrounding circumstances such as proximity to bases, or staging posts, the depth of water which makes submarine and mining operations more or less feasible, the availability of shore-based air power, and a number of others. Some 'feel' for what this startling (and for the West rather alarming) reversal of the offensive/defensive ratio means in practice, may however be deduced from the level of current deployments in the Indian Ocean. This has stabilised over the last year or so, and in round figures some 55 Allied ships have been deployed to maintain what is considered to be adequate power to deter or contain the 27 ships normally on station in the Soviet Indian Ocean squadron.

In the light of these rough numerical comparisons, and the need for maritime defensive forces substantially to exceed those of an aggressor, the ability of the Allies and the West to achieve their primary and secondary objectives, must, *outside the NATO area* and certainly if they were the only criteria, be regarded as slender. To these disadvantages must be added the trend, already remarked and which started in about 1978, for Soviet new construction, particularly of the larger classes of ship (including amphibious assault ships), to overtake that of the combined Western and more specifically NATO navies. In particular, the failure of successive Administrations in the United States to order replacement attack carriers, large and small escort vessels and sea control ships in good time, must mean that even if ordered now they will hardly be commissioned for service in this decade. The same may be said, *mutatis mutandis,* of the failure of Her Majesty's Government (almost entirely for economic rather than doctrinaire reasons) to keep the numbers of modern anti-submarine escorts up to the necessary strength for the task before them. For though a *comparison* of numbers at sea does not mean very much in weighing the chances of success or failure it must be only too clear that the sheer size and scope of the potential world-wide battlefield, coupled with the need for the defence to outnumber significantly the attacker, must imply a certain minimum number of each class of ship if any confidence is to be felt within NATO in the outcome of a clash.

One specialised area which could be of profound (though not decisive) importance in a war at sea, is mining and mine countermeasurers. The Allies have very little capability for laying mines, which it may be remarked can be done easily and cheaply by surface ships (not necessarily warships), by aircraft and by submarines. The kit required is simple and easy to fit, and the skill to operate it is minimal, because both the sophistication and the corresponding menace of almost every modern mine lies in the weapon itself. The small Allied capability in this field flows deliberately and directly from what has already been said about the Soviet merchant fleet, and the fact that while it is 'nice for them to have', mainly as an economic weapon of considerable power in peace time, it is not needed to provide them with the sinews of war. The contrary is equally obviously true, for the West, of the Atlantic Bridge and the immensely long sea lines of trade and supply, and it is no surprise to learn that the Soviets are estimated to maintain a peace establishment of about half a million mines with which to destroy traffic at each end of that vital Bridge, or such as may successfully negotiate the longer transit from outside the NATO area. What is relevant, and alarming, to the outcome of a land-air battle in Europe rather than to the naval war in its support, is that the Allies today are woefully short of mine countermeasures vessels. Numbers here are of the essence, and the requirements can be calculated with some precision given even conservative estimates of the threat; there is no doubt at all that all the ports of the United Kingdom, and those of our friends with coast lines in the Mediterranean, the Channel, the Baltic approaches and the North Sea, are highly vulnerable to mining. Without exaggerating the danger, it should not be forgotten that every Soviet or Bloc merchantman (all of which are as centrally controlled and directed from Soviet naval headquarters as are their warships) is capable of laying mines on passage to and from Allied ports in time of 'peace'.

If the Soviets should start hostilities, then what would be its likely course? The very breadth of the possibilities must be confined at once by some reasonable assumptions, viz: we are looking at a war at sea, not of such a short duration as may be measured in days, and while nuclear weapons may be used on, over or under the sea, it is not part of a general nuclear war. To these must be added, for this purpose only, the further explicit assumption that fighting at sea will only break out following a period of rising tension, which in itself implies political and operational indicators, almost certainly accompanied by economic pressures sufficiently unusual to point in the same direction.

During this (assumed) period of rising tension each side will obviously do its utmost to maximise its order of battle by bringing ships forward from reserve, curtailing and completing repairs and refits, accelerating new construction, calling up reservists and the like, so that it follows that by the time battle is joined all those vessels, and maritime aircraft fit to fight will be ready to do so. Naval control of shipping measures in the general sense of centrally controlled routeing and the activation of dormant plans for convoys and their escorts will, in the West have been made ready and the retired and reserve people trained in peace for this major undertaking will be in post. On the Soviet side their merchant fleet will have been recalled to home ports, or to those of neutrals expected to be benevolent, almost certainly having laid such mines as they may be carrying in the approaches to Allied naval bases as well as commercial ports and harbours. Some ships may have been requisitioned from trade for auxiliary duties, for example, in the United Kingdom, trawlers for mine-sweeping and bigger vessels for logistic duties. World wide communications between naval headquarters, commercial bases and ships at sea, will have been put on a war footing and dormant coding procedures introduced. Spares and all forms of logistic support for the fighting fleets will have been built up as high as possible, and dispensed not only to normal naval bases but to such pre-selected forward operating bases as can be made ready. Most of this quite long catalogue applies largely to the West, and there are as many other preparations (some obviously secret) which have not been listed, but would have been put in hand or completed. The same huge administrative problem does not, certainly in principle, apply to the Soviet Navy, for their bases and ports are in the homeland save for a few in surrogate countries such as those in Africa, Cuba and Vietnam. Nor is there much realistic probability that their seaborne forces (except for submarines) would be able to return to their home bases for re-arming, replenishment, or repair, and this accounts for their emphasis in the last decade on afloat support of all kinds, in which they have made great progress, though have probably not yet reached the level of Western naval expertise in this field.

Such considerations as these point clearly enough to two respectable, if hypothetical, preliminary conclusions which are first, that both sides will fight, and win or lose or draw, with what they have when the battle is joined. There will be no time for new construction (except such as is already in an advanced stage of completion) to affect the orders of battle on either side. Nor will the output of armament industries be susceptible to such expansion as to increase significantly the stocks held at the outset. The second is that the comparatively readier, and much more widespread, access to friendly bases enjoyed by the Western navies should be strongly to their advantage, the longer the conflict endures. An advantage of this nature could, of course, be cancelled by a really huge superiority in numbers, but though Mr Willmott has shown that the

Soviets would bear ship losses much more readily than could the West (because they have no critical oceanic interests and regard ships as expendable anyway), it has been shown that while the offence/defence ratio is much in their favour, the gross superiority required in numbers does not at present exist. It may be added, almost parenthetically, that it seems in general terms inconceivable that a war at sea, limited by our assumptions, could continue for more than a few months at the very most, without spreading to the land or being tacitly regarded as a draw.

However that may be, we may now assume that after a period of rising tension hostilities begin. It seems highly probable that they would do so outside the NATO area, and equally probable that rather than a dramatic all-out world wide attack on all Allied shipping (and even neutrals bound for Allied ports) sporadic sinkings, widely spread geographically would be the first hard signal. From a Soviet point of view there is everything to be said for such a tactic: it is certainly less likely to lead quickly to escalation on land, it would greatly complicate the deployment of Allied maritime forces, as the example of the current numbers opposed in the Indian Ocean makes starkly clear. It would probably be hoped to lead, certainly in the early days, to a withdrawal of units, even if it were not on a large scale, from the protection of the North Atlantic. It would, equally probably, pay NATO forces best to remain fully deployed to guard that vital bridge, once it became clear that a war, rather than incidents at sea had begun, though the political consequences of abandoning our non-NATO friends would be as gravely worrying as would the material consequences to Western Europe and North America of leaving the ocean highways, with their truly vital cargoes, less well guarded. The most practical solution, which also seems to be the most likely, would be for the West in general and NATO in particular to leave their deployments much as they have evolved at the outbreak of hostilities. A tolerable level of protection of the Indian Ocean and South Atlantic can be afforded by the Allied ships on those stations, more particularly if strenuous efforts have been successfuly made for *ad hoc* support from the navies of South Africa and South America.

Very soon the primary objectives of both sides must inevitably be put to the test in the Battle of the Atlantic Bridge (a name coined simply to distinguish it from the two Battles of the Atlantic already fought). There can be hardly any doubt that it would be, like them 'a damned close-run thing'. It will be won or lost by the side which can deny the areas of sea - which will constantly shift and change - to the other. There can be no doubt that every available Soviet attack submarine will be on station, but there can equally be no doubt that thanks to permanently

151

emplaced sea-bed detection devices (which the Soviets neither have nor need) the whereabouts of most of them will be well enough known. NATO's attack submarines, though less numerous, will be close on their heels, and it should not be assumed that this first line of defence will be less than effective. Certainly the numbers game comes closer to the front of the picture than it did, for compared with the days when Doenitz's 50 U-boats were faced by some 25 aircraft carriers and 800 escorts and 1,000 maritime aircraft, the balance looks dauntingly less favourable today. This points clearly to a two-phase sea denial strategy for the NATO navies, in the first of which every resource must be devoted to the 'hunt and kill' operation. This is now, to an extent undreamt of in the Second World War, a team affair which includes surface ships, attack submarines, helicopters with their own sonar and homing weapons, and maritime aircraft similarly equipped but with much greater range, endurance, and weapon load. It seems probable, and realistic too, to suppose that it is in this first desperate phase that 'aptitude' will play a leading part, made up of combat experience, carefully refined and endlessly practiced tactics, leadership, and that final intangible always available to any defender which the French have illuminated by their phrase 'ils ne passeront pas'. Successive Supreme Allied Commanders Atlantic have believed that their job can be done, but they also believe it will be a desperate business with heavy losses, and that their other two jobs of securing the flow of suppy and re-inforcement traffic across that bridge, and of providing air support for the Northern Flank and even the Central Region, cannot be started until the first is successfully completed. One of these distinguished Commanders has publicly lamented that he has a three-job mission and a one-job Fleet to do it with, and he is right. This seems, on the whole, a realistic assessment of the possible course and outcome of the initial sea denial objective of both sides, though there can be no certainty either way.

After the inevitably heavy losses on both sides (which cannot be made good), the second crucial phase must start. This, too, is essentially a sea-denial operation for both sides, though it is important to have constantly in mind that what has to be protected (by NATO) or sunk (by the Soviets) are ships, and not the lanes or corridors or even areas along or through which they must pass. This, for once, simplifies the problems for the defence and makes it more difficult for the attacker. Nevertheless the received wisdom seems generally accepted to be that what the Americans call the 'roll-over' technique is the best way of protecting ships in such a situation. This implies powerful and balanced escort groups, which include all members of the anti-submarine team already mentioned, but augmented by anti-air and anti-surface specialist forces, rolling-over the Atlantic, area by area, to provide a safe and clear passage for the convoys which will now begin to use the Bridge.

The success, or failure, by NATO to keep traffic moving in both directions along that Bridge will be very directly affected by the respective attrition rates during the first 'hunt and kill' phase of the campaign. These, as has been said, are certain to be heavy on both sides. The second phase will start with the ships, aircraft and submarines which are left and still able to operate effectively. It is, at this point, rather than at the outset, that the 'numbers game' will have a decisive influence on the outcome. It has been shown, and the tabular analysis makes clear, that the combined strength of the NATO navies, measured in numbers of hulls, must be regarded today as marginal for the task in hand, and this is the aspect of the future which causes the most concern in the minds of Allied naval Commanders, and their planners alike.

On the other side of the coin it seems likely that Allied strategy and tactics in the bitter opening struggle for the control (and thus denial to the Soviets) of areas of sea, will have held back the American attack carriers with their organic air power, and their own anti-submarine and anti-aircraft defences. There is also likely to have been rather low attrition of NATO's shore-based maritime air, and of their extensive chain of passive and permanently emplaced sea-bed early warning devices. These latter features, and especially the carrier-borne tactical air power now to be brought into play, should bolster the effectiveness of the 'roll-over' technique.

The Battle of the Atlantic Bridge will, in such hypothetical circumstances, begin to look much more like the second Battle of the Atlantic, and it seems probable that its ebb and flow will follow a similar pattern. The major changes, of supreme importance to the Commanders on both sides, will arise from the dramatic technological advances made in the intervening forty years, whose main effect will be enormously to increase the range and the speed at which the previously rather slow moving close actions were fought. Submarines now go much faster and deeper and can detect (by passive means which do not give away their position) surface ships at ranges increased by a factor of at least ten. Moreover, the nuclear powered attack submarine need never surface and is thus immune to radar detection. In the same way shore-based long range Soviet naval aircraft can cover the whole of the North Atlantic (and other oceans too from forward operating bases in East and West Africa), and are armed with anti-ship missiles which are effective at 'stand-off' ranges of 200 miles or more. On the defensive side of the coin and thus from NATO's point of view, the anti-submarine 'team' already listed has stretched its detection range to a corresponding degree, through the use

153

of hunter-killer submarines, as well as ship-borne helicopters with three or four times the speed and range of surface ships. Helicopters' detection and location equipment in nearly all respects is as effective as the sonars mounted in frigates or destroyers, and they are armed with homing anti-submarine missiles (torpedoes is by now a misnomer for them) which are a match for any fast deep-diving submarine. Finally, in these scales, must be weighed the long range weapons now carried by surface escorts and their ability, through sophisticated computers, to share all the information available from every source on both the under-water and air borne threats. This leads to the conclusion that the means available to each side in the second phase of sea control are broadly matched, with, through their superior detection capability, probably a slight edge in favour of NATO. Whether this will be enough to balance the undoubted shortage in numbers of escorts, only the battle itself would show. Certainly neither side, on the evidence, would be wise to embark on this dramatic undertaking confident of victory, much less an easy one.

Should it come to pass, which must seem on the face of it somewhat unlikely, there can be no doubt that it would be as bitter, and lead to as many heavy losses on both sides as that in the first phase. It would seem, on the facts and likely projections, that the duration and intensity of the 'hunt and kill' operations (which could hardly reach a conclusion one way or the other in less than two or three months) would be such as to lead to the declaration of a draw - expressed of course in suitable lapidary political formulae - or an escalation to land-air war in Europe.

SELECTED BIBLIOGRAPHY

Burke. A. SOVIET SEA POWER. (Georgetown University, 1969.)
Dismukers. B. and McConnell J. SOVIET NAVAL DIPLOMACY. (Pergamon. 1979.)
Dull. P. S. A BATTLE HISTORY OF THE IMPERIAL JAPANESE NAVY. (U.S.N.I. 1978.)
Herrick, R. W. SOVIET NAVAL STRATEGY. (U.S.N.I. 1968.)
Hezlet. A. THE SUBMARINE AND SEA POWER. (Davis. 1967.)
Hezlet. A. THE AIRCRAFT AND SEA POWER. (Davis. 1970.)
Lewis. M. THE HISTORY OF THE BRITISH NAVY. (Pelican. 1956.)
Mahan. A. T. THE INFLUENCE OF SEA POWER UPON HISTORY. 1660-1783.
    (University Paperbacks. 1965.)
Mallmann Showell. J. P. THE GERMAN NAVY IN WW2. (Arms and Armour Press. 1979.)
MccGwire. M. SOVIET NAVAL DEVELOPMENTS. (Praeger. 1973.)
MccGwire. M., Booth K. and McDonnell. J. SOVIET NAVAL POLICY. (Praeger. 1975.)
MccGwire, M. and McDonnell. J. SOVIET NAVAL INFLUENCE. (Praeger. 1977.)
Preston. A. U-BOATS. (Bison. 1978.)
Polmar. N. SOVIET NAVAL POWER. (N.S.I.C. 1972.)
Rosinski. H. THE DEVELOPMENT OF NAVAL THOUGHT. (N.W.C. 1977.)
Roskill, S. W. THE WAR AT SEA. (Three volumes; four parts.) (H.M.S.O. 1954-61.)
Roskill. S. W. THE STRATEGY OF SEA POWER. (Collins. 1963.)
Roskill. S. W. THE NAVY AT WAR. (Collins. 1964.)
Wegener. E. THE SOVIET NAVAL OFFENSIVE. (U.S.N.I. 1975.)

Periodicals and Journals

DEFENCE
FLIGHT INTERNATIONAL
INTERNATIONAL DEFENCE REVIEW
NAVY INTERNATIONAL
PROCEEDINGS OF THE U.S. NAVAL INSTITUTE
R.U.S.I. JOURNAL
THE MILITARY BALANCE
THE STRATEGIC SURVEY
JANE'S FIGHTING SHIPS

INDEX OF SHIPS AND CLASSES
listed by country and alphabetically

Notes:
1 Name ship and class treated synonymously, but other ships of class are listed individually without reference to class.
2 Dates, either of launch or when mentioned in text, are only given to differentiate between ships of the same name and type.

November (class of fleet submarine) 108
Petropavlovsk (CG) 119
Quebec (class of submarine) 105
Romeo (class of submarine) 105
S-13 (submarine) 103ref.
Skoryi (class of destroyer) 105
Stalingrad (projected heavy cruisers) 105, 109
Sverdlov (class of cruiser) 102, 106, 109

Tashkent (CG) 119
Typhoon (SSBN?) 120
Victor (class of fleet submarine) 108
Whisky (class of submarine) 105
Whisky Longbin (class of SSG) 108
Yankee (class of SSBN) 108, 130
Zulu (class of submarine) 105, 106
Zulu-V (class of SSG) 108, 110

Notes:

1 In the interests of simplicity the term 'battleship' has been used to cover ships that should be termed 'line-of-battle ships'.
2 Most navies called their first-generation submarines 'Hollands' but this name has been included only in the American list.

INDEX OF NATIONS

GENERAL INDEX